UNSTOPPABLE

THE RISE OF FEMALE GLOBAL LEADERS

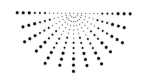

AMA PUBLISHING   PEN CROWN PUBLISHING

CONTENTS

FOREWORD

We are never done transforming. That's actually what makes us unstoppable. We continue on a journey and don't arrive. How exciting that the curiosity and learning remain alive in us—the sourdough starter of our minds and souls. Especially if we feed it; especially if we don't yield to complacency; especially if we don't accept without question the patterns of messaging that have insidiously informed our interactions and that may not be serving our whole being.

The everyday superpower of negotiation is a transformative power that too many women, in particular, have not yet harnessed. Negotiation isn't just for business; it's everybody's business. It's all around us every day from the bedroom, to the kitchen, to our kids' school, to the boardroom. If you haven't tapped into your everyday negotiation superpowers, there's great news: you have it. It's analog. It's portable. You can hone it, and it can transform your everyday life to something where you confidently show up in every aspect.

Unstoppable? Pause-able, at times. That's what makes you so stealth: those moments of reflection, of reassessment, and of recovery from getting knocked down. And then you'll keep showing up, maybe not in the same place but a different place (knowing when to walk away doesn't stop you; it's a wisdom that, ultimately, propels you forward). Anyone who's been a parent understands that progress is not linear. The unstoppable part of you isn't that you never falter or that you "win" at everything. It's that you are an insatiable learner. Always improving, never arriving. Like an asymptote.

May you never finish transforming.

S. Lucia Kanter St. Amour

VP Emerita UN Women San Francisco; Attorney; Author of For the Forces of Good: The Superpower of Everyday Negotiation

1

DR. ALEXANDRA MCDERMOTT

YOU ARE UNSTOPPABLE

She was the only one who knew how to resuscitate me.
You should never depend on a child to do that for you.
It is the Universe working in reverse.

— DR. ALEXANDRA MCDERMOTT

---

*W*hen you read through the stories in this amazing collection, you may see themes that resonate with **you:** empowerment, grief, triumph, pain, hope, despair, bravery, torment, courage, defeat, resilience, anxiety, grit, isolation, victory, anguish, success, achievement, and so on... the pages in this collection are marked with women who tell their stories vulnerably, with their soul first and heart open.

I was excited to launch this collaborative book collection. I knew I wanted to gather women leaders throughout the world to share their stories in this way. They were excited too. I met with each woman leader to understand her impetus for sharing her story now.

As I met with them, they shared similar sentiments:

I want women to understand they are not alone, no matter what they face.

I want women to know they can do it, regardless of their circumstances.

I want women to know, no matter what age they are, they can change their life.

I want women to know how they see other women, especially online, is not their story.

I want women to read my story so they know what rock bottom looks like—I want them to know there is a way out.

I loved the vulnerability of each of these women leaders. I was honored when we discussed the types of messages they wanted to share with the world. I was thrilled when I saw how connected they had become to one another throughout the process, from all corners of the world, once strangers, now bonded through shared lived experiences.

I knew then that I had not only found my purpose in life, it was solidified.

In Sharing My Story Now I Learned More About Myself:

RESEARCH DOES NOT ALWAYS YIELD THE ANSWER

I have declared in other books that I am a researcher to my very core. It is my "go-to." Here, I did what I always do and I researched the first use of the word "Unstoppable." What I came to learn was it was allegedly first used by Theodore Hook in 1836. I did more research. I even read an e-book about Hook to figure out where he used it and how. I chased a ton of rabbit holes. I could not find where "Unstoppable" was first used, and in what context, only that Hook allegedly first used it.

If you seek to define "Unstoppable" as an adjective, you will learn that it means "that cannot be stopped or surpassed; unbeatable." The definitions from the various lexicons online are virtually the same. When you perform further research on the word, you will learn that many people over the years have used it as word to define their programs, charities, and mindsets; it is even a song by Sia.

When I reflected deeply on my life, during my transformative years, starting in 2022, what I came to realize was that no matter what was happening to me at the time, I never stopped. Even in my deepest moments of despair, I kept moving. This, I believe, is the essence of the word Unstoppable. Thus, if we deeply reflect on the word and its definition, if we each keep moving, even slightly, we are all *Unstoppable*.

THE IMPACT OF STORYTELLING AND THE ART OF INTENTION

I have three published stories in three different book collaborations, which serve as part of what I have come to define "my transformative story." Every time I have published a story, I have made choices in that story regarding what details I should print.

Every time an author shows up in print, the author makes a series of choices. In my case, there are so many parts of my life that I wish to share with the world because I know it would make a difference in your life. However, for many reasons I simply cannot share those details. Thus, as a storyteller, I must make choices. I must decide what details I can share to make the biggest impact on your life. I want to ensure that the details I share serve as the platform for you to be able to change your life. I want your dreams to come true. I want you to understand you are in control of your life. You can set your vision for a fulfilling, happy life. You can create the life of your dreams.

With these sentiments in mind, I will share the parts of my transformative story that may allow these doors to open for you now and for this to happen for you.

SIGNIFICANT PIVOTAL MOMENTS IN MY TRANSFORMATIVE STORY FROM 2022-2023

As I am writing this chapter, it has been over a year since I have been uncoupled. Our divorce was final on November 20, 2023. I was with my ex-husband for more than half of my life, almost 26 years.

MY DAUGHTER BECAME MY SAVIOR

I have six children. They have always asked over the years who I love more, so I will just state it up front: I love you equally, but for different reasons. I truly have a different relationship with each of them and our relationships have transformed over the years, depending on where I lived, where they lived, and what was happening at the time.

At the end of my relationship with my ex-husband, we lived in Texas. This is an important detail, as we moved around the country for most of my adult life. We lived in California, Minnesota, California, Georgia, California, and then Texas. Even in California we moved from house to house about every two or three years.

We had a 36-acre ranch in Texas. We loved the serenity it provided. My ex-husband chose the property. We had narrowed our purchase down to two properties and he won. I was okay with it though. It was a beautiful property. It was quiet and serene. We had an asphalt driveway that was gated, and our property had barbed-wire fencing around the whole thing. It had a tiny pond, small green pastures, a huge tan shop, and a two-story home with a wrap-around porch and plenty of room for our family.

After about a year, we eventually purchased a second property an hour away. It is a stunning log cabin that we still own. I decorated it myself. I chose every piece of furniture that went into it. I even found a woodcarver and re-did the staircase. I had custom furniture built and asked the woodcarver to transform the trunk of one of our trees into a wood carving spirit.

Through many conversations, I asked my oldest daughter to move from Georgia to Texas. I think I finally broke her down and she agreed. Eventually she moved with her partner into a shop at the back of the property at the Log Cabin. We eventually turned the Log Cabin into a rental property, and she began managing it for us. She was doing a stellar job. She would visit me on our ranch when my ex-husband was not home. Her relationship with him was strained due to how he would direct her on the rental property and a few other things.

I remember her coming over to the ranch and asking to speak with me in my office. She was seventeen at the time.

"My office" had become my safe haven. It was a room off our master bedroom. We had stuffed the odd pieces of furniture into it. We added a fold-out blue queen sofa bed couch in case we had too many guests stay with us. We inherited a few glass oak cabinets from the homeowner before us that we kept on one wall, and it had a built-in desk and bookshelf in the corner. We added an old television, a stand-up game I purchased from Best Buy, and eventually it stored some of my Poshmark things I listed for sale.

My ex-husband had an office of his own that was connected to our house. It was a place he re-did for himself. It had cedar-lined walls, and my father's executive desk and chair. He had two computers, safes, a refrigerator in case he was thirsty, and his walls were covered in art.

I remembered how my daughter looked at me. Our connectedness is soul-deep.

"Mama... the behavior must change," and she took me by both hands.

The conversation did not feel rehearsed, so something must have triggered her, I thought.

My first reaction was to defend myself: "I am not sure you understand what is at stake here, baby."

"No, mama. I actually do."

"Look, baby, I have thought so much about this—I know what happens if I leave—I have to think about your baby sisters."

My oldest daughter is an empath to her core. I knew she had walked through every scenario as I had already. She knew the stakes and what was at issue—she felt the clouds of darkness, cruelty, manipulation, deceit, lying, anxiety, despair, and anguish.

"Mama, if the behavior does not change by the time you turn 50 years old, I will pack your things myself."

Her words landed on me like a 2,000-pound weight at that moment. I felt bricks falling on my shoulders from every corner of the sky. My body heated up. My feet numbed. I flushed. I was not angry at all. I absorbed the weight. I was present. I listened. I heard her, thanked her, and we hugged. We left my office, and she went home.

I reflected for days on her words. I crafted every scenario in my mind of how I might exit the marriage. In my heart, I knew he was unfaithful but had no proof yet. I was triaging multiple crises with my undiagnosed medical condition, six children and their crises, and a failing marriage I could not, and maybe did not, want to fix. All I knew for sure is I was unhappy to my core and I did not know how to fix anything.

PHYSICAL SYMPTOMS CAN BE A WAKE-UP CALL

For many years, I experienced different kinds of physical pain. My ex-husband brushed it off when I would try and share it with him. I remember one time, when he came home from one of his trips, I was excited to see him, but I could not leave the bed. I heard the door open and close. He entered our bedroom, and I was on our bed working on my computer. He looked at me and rolled his eyes. I had not seen him for a week.

At one point, even though I was teaching at a Tier One research university, he told me "to get a real job." He was always throwing verbal stones at me. A long time ago when we were roughly on par with each other career-wise, we had a very serious discussion with respect to whose career we would support. At that time, I was working as a civil litigator at a law firm and trying to become their first female partner. We had three children under the age of five. We decided it was best to support his career. Afterwards, I pivoted several times in my career, furthered my education, and took flexible roles to support his career aspirations, which required us moving around the country.

One night, I remember waking up from a pain so intense in my abdomen it can only be described as being squeezed like a vice. I popped up from a dead sleep. I sat still like a statue and thought to myself: *Oh, my G-d, I am going to be paralyzed.* I could barely breathe. My ex-husband was snoring next to me. I tried taking deep shallow breaths. The pain was so intense every time I breathed in it felt like an electric shock through my abdomen. I held my breath. I picked a place on the wall in front of me with only the moonlight to help guide me and prayed to G-d. Praying was not something I was in the habit of doing at the time. I had lost faith in G-d after my mother passed away of pancreatic cancer. My connection to G-d was strained after my mother died and I really did not know how to get my connection back. Through muffled short breaths I muttered: *Please. I can't breathe. I don't know what's happening to me. Please help me.* Tears started rolling down my cheeks. My shallow breaths continued. The electrical pain shot through my whole body. I closed my eyes. I tried to take a deeper breath. The pain started disappearing. After a couple of minutes, it was gone.

I always worked on my computer in my bedroom, propped up on my black, fuzzy, collegiate back pillow—the ones you send your kid off to college with as they embark on their years of academic study. I asked my twins to take a shower, which was customary before going to school. They preferred taking a shower in my bathroom because it was bigger and "more fun." Apparently, they had emerged from the shower, kissed me, and went to their room. Fifteen minutes later I called their names and asked them to take a shower. Surprised and somewhat curious they came back into my room, looked at me perplexed and said, "Mama, we literally took a shower, kissed you, and went to our room." I was stunned—but not surprised. I had been experiencing weird bouts of memory loss for months, which is why I had spoken with my university and asked them to basically retire me. I could no longer show up for my students the way they needed me to be. It was getting worse. Now, I started to panic.

There were times when I was driving in the car and my toes would lock up. I had to pull the car over and physically take off my shoe and unfurl my toes. There were times I could no longer feel my fingers or my hands or my feet. There were times I had to throw my legs off the bed to simply get out of bed in the morning to take my girls to school or to pick them up from school. The doctors began testing me for Multiple Sclerosis and the results were inconclusive.

I was experiencing physical symptoms I could not explain and each day they were getting worse. I had no one to tell, no support from my ex-husband, and no doctor could explain them. I felt trapped in my body and the physical pain was getting worse by the day. I had no idea from one day to the next what symptoms would appear or what would happen to me. I started to anticipate that something would happen I could not explain and I was not ready for it physically, emotionally, mentally, or spiritually. I was finally broken.

I started crying on the shower floor every morning and some-times in the evening. At times my body would get so cold; only hot water would heat it up. I got myself into the fetal position on the shower floor and let the hot water cover my back and eventually pool over my body and skin. This way, no one saw me cry, and no one shared my suffering.

Even though she lived an hour away, there was one person who felt it and knew it to her core: my oldest daughter.

FROM ONE LIFE TO ANOTHER: SHE BROUGHT ME BACK

I was determined to have a baby girl. We did IVF twice. We were informed as they implanted four eggs in me that there was a possibility that a couple would take, or that maybe none of them would take—I did not care. I wanted my baby girl. She was strong and born on time.

We named her intentionally too. Her name means "blooming and verdant" and her middle name represents "wide open fields."

As a child, she was remarkable. She looked at life with wild abandon. Her hair was corkscrew curly with a blond-golden tint and she galloped everywhere with a smile on her face. She was drawn to nature, being outside, picking flowers, and dancing in the wind. She had no fear of living creatures or dead things either. She once found a dead bird outside and carried it inside to show us. She was incensed that it was no longer alive and somehow in her little mind I think she thought she could still save it. We asked her politely to take it back outside and tried to explain to her it was no longer alive. Unfortunately, she lost track of the dead bird inside the house. We found it a couple of days later on the fireplace mantle.

She laughed all day and learning new things inspired her so school was not a chore but a gift. Eventually, we had her tested and her IQ was off the charts. I had experience with giftedness before as her brothers had skipped a grade in school already and we had managed to come up with a plan to keep them engaged. But she was different and a new challenge emerged. I became the problem. As an attorney, I had been exposed to many cases in my life that created a protection in me that I could not deny. Now, I had a baby girl.

I remember the day I picked her up from her first day at school. The teacher asked to speak with me. I thought: *Oh no, what happened.*

"Can I have a word with you?"

These are never the words you want to hear from anyone at your children's school.

"Of course. Please."

"It is about your daughter. We asked her to use the bathroom with the other kids and she said *no*. She has not used the bathroom the whole day."

I knew immediately what happened.

The day before she went to school, I had a heart-to-heart with my amazing, fearless six-year-old daughter. I told her that really not everyone in the world had the best of intentions. She needed to be mindful and careful. She needed to watch her surroundings. She needed to have heightened awareness. She needed to protect herself.

I did not realize that our "heart-to-heart" must have created an unrelenting anxiety in her that she refused to go to the bathroom with anyone. She was following my instructions and heeding my words.

We actually talk about this now. I have apologized to her profusely. She laughs and tells me that it set her up for success in life. This is her mindset. She tells me that she now has incredible vigilance and is keenly aware of her surroundings and what is happening around her at all times.

One night she and her partner were at our house. My ex-husband was home too. I had a feeling it would be a particularly difficult evening. He had just come home from a trip. I begged her and her partner to stay over at the house. They agreed and said they would watch movies on the couch in the family room.

My ex-husband and I decided to have a conversation in our bedroom. He exclaimed how "unhappy" he was and did not know how to fix it. He called me a failure. He started referring to his phone and quoting things from our past fights over the past several months, to probably a year. He told me how he had been seeing a therapist and it was not working. He was just "unhappy." Tears streamed down my face. *I could not believe he called me a failure.* When he saw me crying, he got angry and said, "There it is—crying. Of course." He could never handle anyone crying in the house. It was an emotion he simply could not understand, embrace, or manage. It was foreign to him. We tried to never cry in front of him. We would subject

16

ourselves to endless ridicule. He followed it up with: "It is an 'Ali-Problem' and I just 'Can't Ali Right Now'." At that moment, I crawled into bed and got under the covers. I was stunned. I truly did not know what to do at all. He had no trouble falling asleep. In minutes he was snoring.

After an hour or so, I decided I was going to take a drive in my car and think. I felt trapped in that room. I saw my daughter and her partner on the couch. My daughter begged to go with me. I told her no and left. I drove around for hours contemplating what to do, where to go, and what my life had become. I knew I could no longer subject myself to that level of cruelty. During my car ride, I recalled various phrases he had told me over the past several months—at one point during one of our fights he told me he just did not think he loved me anymore, he denied being in a relationship with anyone else, he told me he was working on showing up as a better husband and a better father. He lied.

When I returned home, my daughter and her partner were awake and on the couch. They hugged me. We all knew what had to happen, but I just had not yet created a path. Her strength and love and silence was all I needed to get through the rest of the night. They ended up leaving before anyone woke up the next morning.

I cannot count the moments when my daughter showed up for me when I needed her the most. I reflect often on her words to me in my office. There are so many moments when she would show up at the house, when I was crying on the shower floor and somehow she knew I needed her love and strength. She was there during the divorce trial, the aftermath, and the move-out. She suffered as much abuse as I did for being there for me and she took it. It was patently unfair. She told the truth. She showed up ethically and morally.

With her love, strength, and grace, she allowed me to channel my own awareness. Each day I felt a little more *Unstoppable*. I would not be where I am today without her helping me clear my path. I often reflect on how it must have felt unfair for a daughter to help her mother like she helped me. I wonder if it felt like an unrelenting burden. It took immense courage and bravery for her to come to me and share her feelings, and even give me an ultimatum. She saw what I could no longer see and she knew how to protect me.

She is now in California and living her life. She lives an hour away and frankly, I do not see her as much as I would like. Any time I have ever needed someone to drop something, she is there. No questions asked. She does it with an open heart, and with love, at a moment's notice.

At times, I can sense from her she feels she is not living her purpose. Her brain is so big. Traditional schooling is not enough for her and her interests are deep. I have been exposed to so many leaders, scholars, academicians, innovators, and changemakers in my life. There is no one like her in the world. I want her to hear this, embrace this, and lean into it.

She has the gift of resuscitation and she brought me back to life.

She is Unstoppable.

THE GIFT OF BEING UNSTOPPABLE

What I came to learn through my reflection is that we are all *Unstoppable.*

It means, literally, that we simply keep moving. We do not stop. It does not take herculean strength. It means in your darkest moments, the times when you think you cannot breathe, take one shallow breath at a time, and do not stop.

There are moments in each of our lives that we can pinpoint that have transformed us forever and made us who we are today. For many of us it involved severe trauma. For others of us, it was like a slow drip that only became recognizable to others who saved us.

What I would love people to understand is that we are all connected through our stories, shared experiences, and most of all, love for one another. As people throughout the world share their lived experiences, authentically, soul first, heart open, unapologetically, it can change someone else's life. As their life changes, so too does their circle of influence. It is the "butterfly effect" in action. It takes one story. One person. One impact. The results are infinite. Our love for each other will change the world.

No matter what happens to you on any given day, you always have a choice. It is a moment in time. A snapshot in history. Tomorrow you will be gifted another day, and another choice to be your best self in that moment. You can decide how you show up in the world and if you do not like your choice, you get another choice tomorrow.

You Are Unstoppable

Do not Despair -
Just close your eyes.

Remember my Dear -
You control your Light.

Take it all in -
It will soon pass.

You will rise again -
And soon you will see

You will open your eyes
become filled with Your Light

Only You control
What comes to be.

Embrace it all -
Your Enormity.

Fill the World
With Your Love
And Your Light –

One breath
One step
One day
At a time.

ABOUT DR. ALEXANDRA MCDERMOTT

Dr. Alexandra McDermott ("Ali") is the CEO of Pen Crown Publishing and McDermott Leadership. She is also an International Bestselling Published Author, Award Winning Global Leader, Motivational Coach, and Speaker.

Ali recently framed 2022 as the most transformative year of her life when her purpose became clear: to help people discover their purpose and lead the life of their dreams.

She has been published in several genres, coached global leaders to go from stuck to unstoppable, and is now devoted to her life's purpose.

Ali coaches authors on how to share their messages of inspiration and empowerment with high impact while creating the legacy they wish to leave in the world—in both collaborative and full-length books.

Ali thrives on connectedness, so please feel free to connect with her on LinkedIn.

> **LinkedIn:** *www.linkedin.com/in/alexandramcdermott-innovation-management-leadership-venturecapital-entrepreneurship-ai*
>
> **Pen Crown Publishing:** *www.PenCrownPublishing.com*
>
> **McDermott Leadership:** *www.McDermottLeadership.com*
>
> **Amazon Author Page:** *www.amazon.com/author/dralexandramcdermott*

2

ADRIANA MONIQUE ALVAREZ

When I hear the word unstoppable, it conjures a gritty image of determination and perseverance. This wasn't how I ever saw myself.

When I left my rural Colorado community at eighteen, I was a scared girl who simply knew she could not stay. I would not stay for a life that didn't interest me. Marrying the neighbor, moving irrigation morning and night, and becoming whomever others approved of.

I had only one thing motivating me and that was my desire to discover who I was outside of my family and small town.

I found myself overseas as a volunteer in places like Myanmar, Albania, and Kenya. It turned out I wasn't many things I thought I was. I was a delicate flower, but I thrived in war-torn and unstable environments. I was spoiled, but also did well without running water or electricity. And I was much more capable than I had ever imagined. I had a knack for problem-solving and I knew I could figure it out, no matter what it was.

In that decade of my life, I actually gave no thought to what I would be when I grew up. I had no plans or desires to go to college, sit in a classroom, and learn theory. I didn't think about what job, business, or career would be mine. I had no five- or ten-year plan. I was deeply in the moment. I was holding babies, playing with kids, and learning new languages. I lived off $300 a month for years. I had little to no access to the internet or any communication outside of my new world.

When I returned to the States after contracting malaria in Africa, I experienced reverse culture shock. Home no longer felt like home. I couldn't figure out where I actually belonged. I remember landing in New York City, everything was moving fast, and I didn't like it. People were walking, talking on cell phones, and shoving mediocre Starbucks pastries in their mouths. I wanted to get back on the plane and go back to slow living.

I distinctly remember a friend from high school calling me to see how I was when these words fell out of her mouth, you must feel so behind. You aren't married, no degrees, and no job. I had been living in a very different world. One where no one was telling me what my life was supposed to look like and reminding me how to stay on the smooth paved road called The American Dream.

I didn't feel behind at all. I felt satisfied with my life and my choices. I had experiences no one could possibly begin to under-stand, and they forged the person I was. I had seen the world and learned what was really important to me. I had never felt behind, until then that is. Suddenly I began to compare my life to others and wondered if I could stomach the rat race that is America.

I met my husband Derek on a blind date not long after this and when we got married I asked him to promise me one thing that he would never get a job. I didn't want to spend the entire day apart, come home tired, eat dinner, watch TV, and do it all again. I wanted to share my life with him, and I wanted to create a good life together. When we started our first business it was really so that we didn't have to work for the man, and we could have a flexible schedule. I don't think we ever thought we would be successful or rich. We were just hoping to not have overdraft fees every month.

Life unfolded and we experienced more than we ever imagined. We built multiple businesses online and off. We had thousands of clients and hundreds of referral partners. I wrote for every major publication in the world including Forbes, HuffPost, and International Living. I was then featured in them all as well. I was interviewed on hundreds of podcasts and my interviews have had over a million downloads. I have been featured on a NYC billboard for a story I wrote. I am a twenty-three-time international best-selling author and USA Today bestselling author. I have created hundreds of trainings and programs. Started one of the most innovative publishing companies in the world. We have traveled extensively and spent five years abroad as a family.

We ticked off the boxes and then some. We had the life we wanted and a family we loved.

About two years ago while I was facilitating a networking group with amazing women from all over the world, I gave the group a question to ponder and then we were going to share our answers with each other. That was the day everything changed for me. My own question made me realize that hitting another goal wasn't going to do it for me. Adding a zero to my income wasn't going to fulfill me. And there was something I was hungry for that wasn't being satisfied.

While I had been back in my small town for two years, living at my grandparent´s house, I really hadn't transitioned to my new life. I had been fighting it. It wasn´t my idea after all. When the world changed in 2020 it became painfully apparent that travel was no longer going to be fun or easy. We made the decision to move to Colorado and put down roots. We went from switching AirBNBs every three months in the Mediterranean to buying land and planting forty fruit trees.

Once again my system was in shock.

Travel had been with me since I was young. It was how I found myself. It had been my constant companion even through marriage, kids, and the loss of a baby. I actually had no idea how to live without it.

And my business, while from the outside was at the pinnacle of success, it was no longer doing it for me. The thing I had created became my cage. I received fifty to a hundred messages a day from raving fans and absolutely crazy haters. I never knew one minute to the next if I was going to be the hero or the villain. That's the thing with success, it is a double-edged sword, and it can trick you into believing that it matters.

Last winter, on a horribly cold and white day, our entire community gathered to celebrate and mourn the life of a man who had impacted so many. I knew if I died that day, very few would be at my funeral. I had made no positive impact on my local community. In fact, most people didn't even know I was back in town.

While creating an international business with clients in 41 countries had at one time made me feel amazing, I realized none of them actually knew me. None of them would bring meals to my family in my absence. None of them. This epiphany rocked me and led to many difficult, but necessary decisions.

I stepped out of CEO of the company I founded, and I began to consider how I could contribute, not to the world, but to my corner of it.

It has not been romantic or a journey I could recommend to others. It was simply my destiny. Every ounce of clarity, certainty, and control was gone. I feared that my best days were behind me. I wished that I could imagine what was around the corner was going to be amazing, but I didn't. I feared it would devour me and that I would lose everything I had worked for.

I sat in my truck sobbing, and I decided to share my deepest fears with Derek and my Dad. They had no answers, and I am sure they shared at least some of my fears, but they said, we are with you no matter what. That was all I needed to know.

I let my identity, my achievements, my possessions, and my life as I had known it, go. I released it all and made peace with however it shook out. I was no longer who I was, and I was not yet who I could become.

I sat in the void and the dark for weeks and then a peace emerged. I still had no idea what my future would look like, but similar to twenty-two-year-old me, I didn't need to know. I didn't need a goal or a five-year plan. I didn't need a single thing in this world to validate my existence.

I could just be.

Today I wake up and an idea comes to me, and I act on it. Sometimes that's making banana chocolate chip bread for my kids, sometimes it's to feature a local women who has an incredible booth at our local farmer´s market. Some days I drive to a sacred canyon and lay on the rocks for hours and others I clean my house.

I am not the poster woman for an Unstoppable Global Leader. I am the reluctant leader. I am the one no one would have ever bet on. I was good and nice. I put everyone ahead of me. I had no confidence in myself. I never had my life on a vision board. I just kept choosing what felt best one day at a time.

I lived my life for many years under the impression that I created it. That I chose it, and I did. But this season feels like there are new rules. I am leaning back, relaxing into it, and seeing what life delivers to me. I get destiny or fate in a way that baffled me before. I have so much less control than I ever wanted to admit and that is actually a huge relief.

The one thing I have complete control over is how much I enjoy the ride. The twists and turns can either be excruciating or exhilarating.

We took the boys to Legoland for their birthdays this year and like any amusement park, at the end of a ride, you can see the photos taken. We would patiently wait for our picture to pop up in the lot of them.

Recently I thought about those photos. Inevitably some of them were snapshots of happy memories, people having the time of their life, while others were images of terror and tears. It is kind of like life.

We are all on the same ride, we all face very similar challenges and experience the spectrum of emotions. We all live, and we all die. Some enjoy it, and others--not so much.

As I willingly sink my roots deep down into the soil my family has been on for generations, I draw up nourishment from the earth herself. I walk our land and take photos of the budding trees that will soon provide peaches that will become cobbler, smoothies, and ice cream. I watch my boys play baseball and get lost in the orange setting sun. I have no lofty goals. I have no desire to lead anyone other than myself. I am here for the mysterious and magical that can only be found in the unknown.

And all the times when I felt like giving up, when I just didn't think I could handle what was being handed to me, what kept me going? What ultimately makes me unstoppable? Hope. The idea that maybe, just maybe something good was about to happen. I didn't want to miss that.

If you are in a tight spot or a complete transition, it won't last forever.

There is always hope. And I hope that keeps you going because, around the next bend, life has something and someone for you. How could we stop knowing that this is a possibility?

ABOUT ADRIANA MONIQUE ALVAREZ

Adriana Monique Alvarez is the CEO and Founder of AMA Publishing. She is an unconventional visionary whose life and business was inspired by a decade of travel and volunteer work around the world. She is a USA Today best-selling author and a 19 time international bestselling author. She is an artist, photographer, and private chef for her husband Derek and two sons Sam and Grant. She is currently living in the middle of nowhere Colorado where she is renovating her grandparents home and learning how to homestead.

Website: *www.amapublishing.co*

3

DR. DESIREE DEL-ZIO

THE TRAIN HAS LEFT THE STATION

*W*hen your life is a train ride, everything can feel off the rails.

Perhaps that sounds a bit dramatic. It was not that EVERYTHING was off the rails, but many things were. I want this story to be about a woman who worked to get the train back on track and create a life of smooth rides and pleasant stops. This is not that story. This is the story of a woman who learned to embrace life's derailments with a bit of hope, a lot of courage, and a healthy amount of grit. But I am getting ahead of myself. Let's start at the beginning when I arrived at "Elation Station."

FIRST STOP: ELATION STATION

This is not one of those train rides that start off the rails. It is quite the opposite. My parents had a strong, loving marriage, and I had two brothers and one sister with whom I had a solid sibling relationship; we loved enough to know we were family and fought enough not to forget it.

We lived in a sprawling five-bedroom colonial-style home

nestled in the tree-lined woods near New York's Long Island Sound. My family was Italian-American, and every Sunday morning, we awoke to the aroma of my mother cooking homemade meatballs and pasta sauce. Sunday evening dinner was plates of spaghetti, Italian bread slathered in butter, and the promise of a week's worth of leftovers.

We celebrated boisterous holiday events that resembled the same menu as Sunday dinner, with the addition of an extended family that believed in speaking louder than reasonably necessary. I had close to a dozen cousins who joined my family of six and graced our home with thunderous but joyful birthdays, Christmases, Thanksgivings, and Easter Sundays. We shared our history, broke bread, and filled the house with tales of immigration and New York's Little Italy. My cousins, my siblings, and I sat with our elbows on the table, chins in our hands, hearing our collective parents tell tales of our great-grandmothers and aunties who made every meal from scratch, partly because they could and partly because it cost a fraction of the processed substitute sold by the "Americaaanz" who knew nothing about the staples of the old country. We were taught who we were and embraced our place in this microcosm of the world where we "belonged."

It was hard not to be elated. However, as you can imagine, the ride went on.

I attended a small parochial school from second to seventh grade. These were critical years in my social development. I learned the hierarchy of small-town friendships, the excitement of crushing on someone new each month, and valuing the people who always stood up for me. And there was no one more loyal than my best friend, Jennifer.

We had frequent play days and swam in the in-ground pool in my backyard, the water cooling our warm, sun-kissed skin. We dove fearlessly into its crystalline wake, competed to see who could stay under the longest, stood in perfectly erect handstands in the shallow end, and flipped into somersaults in the deep end. We took strolls in the lush green woods behind my house, rode ten-speed bikes briskly up and down the cul-de-sac, and sat on the pink shag rug of my bedroom, playing with Barbies, and sharing dreams of a future we could only barely imagine.

As we grew older, we sneaked samples of my mother's Elizabeth Arden and Maybelline pink blush, sky blue eye shadow, and crimson lipstick to paint our faces. We wandered the trek from her house to the local convenience store, where we bought Tootsie Rolls and blow pops that were all but gone after devouring them on our ten-minute return trip home. Our regular sleepovers never included much sleep.

We were girls growing up in the 80s era; we wore florescent green leg warmers and tied our long brown hair into multi-colored banana clips. We were awed at Eddie Murphy and Dan Aykroyd in "Trading Places" on the big screen and boasted about being among the first to rewind movies on our cutting-edge VCRs.

We showed up to school in our gray and black plaid catholic school uniforms, white button-up shirts, and red bow ties. Our school-day regalia, designed to create a sense of uniformity, permitted us only one unique characteristic: our shoes. We donned them with friendship pins, which were little more than safety pins lined with rainbow beads, fastened to our laces. A simple yet powerful representation of our adolescent connection, they clung to our Keds and Buster Browns, jingling down the hallway, symbolizing our youthful solidarity. It was childhood joyfulness, innocence personified, an easy and blissful existence that included pizza from a locally owned "hole in the wall" for breakfast and Breyer's Mint chocolate chip ice cream for dinner. It was ideal. And then it all changed.

SECOND STOP: DEVASTATION STATION

It was mid-December, and in the early 1980s in New York, that means cold weather, leafless trees, holiday decorations, and, in my house, Jets Football. That weekend, my father, a season ticket holder, offered to take me and Jennifer to a game. I can still hear the crowd's roar and feel the cold air on my skin. We wandered the stands and stuffed our mouths with soda and nachos. We decided which players we thought looked best in their uniforms and talked about being cheerleaders one day. Needless to say, we did not watch much football. But we were together, and at twelve years old, that was all that mattered.

That evening, we dropped her back at her house. I recall stepping out of the car and hugging her. She said, "Love ya," and I responded in-kind. I watched her walk to her front stoop and turn around to wave as she stepped in the doorway. I can still see her. She wore dark blue Jordache jeans, a billowy white sweater, a waist-long black winter coat, and white Reebok sneakers. She smiled, and I smiled back. It was the last time I ever saw her.

The next day was a Sunday, and through the fragrance of our simmering dinner, I picked up our sunflower yellow rotary phone and dialed Jennifer's all too familiar numbers. Her mother answered but had no idea where she was. They had gone to church that morning, and Jennifer, still clad in her "Sunday best," walked the 400 yards from her house to the local convenience store alone, a walk she and I had taken many times. I recalled every step. The busy highway beside us, the high green grass gracing our tube-socked legs, and the artificial neon lights of the convenience store promising aisles of makeup we were not permitted to buy and Snickers and suckers on which we spent our weekly allowance.

Her mother spoke anxiously, telling me that she had not yet returned. I called again a few hours later, and I could hear the panic in her voice. No one had seen Jennifer since she left the convenience store, a mere ten-minute walk away. Her mother promised to have her call me when she got home. She never called.

The following day, while I was asleep, the phone rang. I picked it up, and it was the principal of our school. She asked how we were, and, in retrospect, I imagine that the lack of emotion in my response indicated that we had not "heard the news." She asked to speak with my mother, and I handed the phone to her and listened to the one-sided conversation, the principal's voice a muffled resonance.

"No, I haven't heard."

"Oh, my goodness."

"Oh, no."

The "news" was not good. My mother insisted I leave the room. I did.

Shortly after that, she beckoned me to return. I entered the room, and the phone rang again. She ignored it. She held me to her, and I looked up, my face on her chest, her eyes looking to the ceiling as though they begged heaven for the right words. She cried softly, her body shook, and as a tear streamed down her face, she quietly uttered, "Jennifer is no longer with us."

I was in shock. I did not initially cry. Nothing had meaning yet. I recall saying, "I knew something terrible happened," as though this information had somehow validated the heaviness and fear over the previous day and night.

The phone rang again.

"I am sorry, Desiree is here; I can't talk about it right now." The phone rang again. My mother spoke the same words. Suddenly, it dawned on me; she was gone, and something dreadful had happened to her. Somewhere on that ten-minute walk, a path we traveled together countless times, where we counted how many licks it took to get to the center of a Tootsie Pop, where we competed for the biggest bubble from our flavorless Blow Pop chewing gum, where we shared stories of a future that would never arrive, her life ended. And the terribleness of that end was enough for my mother to shield from me.

It was surreal. It was otherworldly. From that moment until many months later, I was outside my body and mind. I breathed, I moved, but I only existed. My life, as I knew it, was over, and what replaced it had no meaning. I was lost. The train that pulled me gently into Elation Station ran headfirst into Devastation Station, and I was off the rails.

THIRD STOP: OBLITERATION STATION

I was almost thirteen years old, and words like sexual assault, abduction, shallow grave, post-mortem ligature marks, and murder entered my lexicon. The quiet, childlike experiences that made up my days were replaced with nausea, tears that seemed to have no end, a deep depression, and a disregard for my own well-being. I did not recognize myself. I did not recognize my life. I could not smile, eat, or care about anything. That day, the day I learned she died, marked the end of my innocence. The train went into autopilot and headed straight for nowhere, and in that nowhere, my depression, unhealed grief, and unresolved trauma operated that train. And in their unrelenting defiance, they thrust me headlong into complete Obliteration.

The adults in my life were not armed with the tools to help me address my trauma. There was no precedence for this in our pristine world. The rhetoric of the time was that children bounce back from "these things" quickly, give her space, and when she stops crying, you will know she is "over it." My parents were lost in their grief and suffering. That is not to say they did not concern themselves with mine—they did—but they had no idea what to do, and that deficit led to inaction.

The small school I attended was left with one lonely outcast: me. My parents transferred me to the local public school at the end of that school year. They believed I could get away from the unending reminders of her life and her death. They were wrong. Her murder case was high profile, and everyone knew we had been friends. My new classmates had questions and thought I had answers. I was thrust into a sort of macabre celebrity. My emotional self was not safe anywhere.

Shortly thereafter, my parents moved us across the country, where no one knew me or her. While these actions seemed like hopeful solutions, in reality, they were a string of new traumas, taking me further away from myself and from the healing I desperately needed. In the absence of that healing came the defensive and coping mechanisms that would define the next twenty years of my life.

With depression, grief, and trauma operating the train and my conscious mind on autopilot, I was now well off the rails. My memory of the immediate aftermath of her death is vague and scattered. I recall glimpses and pictures of the funeral, the grave site, teachers and other students, my parents' deeply desperate eyes, and my siblings' efforts to "make me feel better." One of my most distinct memories is my bedroom ceiling and the shape of the lampshade's shadow upon it. I realize now this memory represents the hours on my bed, lying on my tear-stained pillow, staring into the oblivion my life had become. Thus began my "acting out" phase that went on for decades.

It started only a few months after her death when I snuck my first drink of alcohol: vodka and orange soda. I had enough to stumble through the day, and when I found my bed, which had become my favorite place to obliviate, I fell into a deep sleep, the first in months. The sweet experience of forced forgetfulness may not have been healing. Still, it felt much better than anything since that fateful morning when "Jennifer was no longer with us."

Thinking had become my least favorite thing to do. It let demons in and kept me filled with darkness. Alcohol offered a gentle reprieve, but at thirteen years old and in a home with parents who did not drink, access became a problem. However, every chance I got, I indulged. When I went away to college, the floodgates opened, and the train happily drove me anywhere I needed to go, which was seldom class and often a party. Promiscuity, substance abuse, and life avoidance were my favorite pastimes, and everyone I surrounded myself with enjoyed the same. We were a bevy of lost souls, all managing a lifetime of hurt with the same debauchery and decadence that efficiently dulled the pain. Hope, self-care, faith, belief, dreams, and goals were safely tucked away in the caboose while I shoved every form of shamelessness into my baggage compartment.

My train sleepwalked me straight into all manner of life evasion, and the Obliteration of my life became the order of the day. I told myself Jennifer's death was a long time ago, and I was over it. There was sufficient evidence to allow me to believe I was right. I managed to graduate college, secure employment, and get married. However, I skated through college, my job was hardly fulfilling, and my marriage was to the one man I could find who was more traumatized than me.

So there I was, a twenty-five-year-old college graduate with a mediocre job, smoking more pot than remotely necessary, and married to a man who secured the first-place ribbon for trauma. Albeit I was a close second. Together, we avoided our distress and acted out all over each other. We fought far more than we loved, and amid our mess-making extravaganza, we bought and sold homes and cars, took vacations, and had two children. Outwardly, we appeared quite ordinary. No one could tell just how off the rails we were, and I was hardly conscious enough to tell them otherwise.

I recall an afternoon when my oldest child was twelve years old, the age I was when Jennifer died. I watched them and their best friend making friendship bracelets on the family room's throw rug, and it dawned on me how innocent they were and how blissfully unaware of humanity's dark underbelly. I realized, through the eyes of an adult, how young I was when my life was ripped apart. I recognized that my train was not on autopilot; it was being driven by a traumatized twelve-year-old girl who needed to heal. I knew it was time to get help. For my children's sake. For my own.

FOURTH STOP: RESTORATION STATION

For the first time in a long time, I had something to live for, my children and the belief that I could change the trajectory of my life. The damage my baggage compartment had accumulated, including my marriage, needed to be addressed. The battle with my past was ending, and the fight for my life was about to begin. And that sounds great, but I had developed a profound expertise in self-destruction, and breaking those habits would become a lifelong effort.

I walked into the serene, dimly lit therapist's office and softly uttered, "When I was twelve years old, my best friend was murdered, and I think it may have affected me." And so it began. I had spent twenty years skating half on and half off the rails, dragging myself along the tracks that led to nowhere. However, I learned that sorting the catastrophic history in my baggage compartment created a storm of new derailments. First, my husband no longer recognized me as I developed emotional perseverance. His partner in trauma and anger was fading away, and as he clutched to our legacy, we grew further apart. We were approaching a fork in the road and no longer going in the same direction. While we had tried couples therapy and counseling, our efforts were fruitless. Eventually, he lost his job, and our financial partnership was broken. Without his income, our lives unraveled quickly, and eventually, my fear that we would lose everything was realized. I knew my marriage was over, and I had to save myself from being pulled into a direction I could no longer travel. Despite my convictions to change, there were no easy choices. I could stay put and live beside a man who did not want to overcome his trauma while I battled with mine, or I could exit our path and take my limping train in another direction. I chose the latter.

At this point, our home, the only home my children knew, was in foreclosure. We had no choice but to leave. I had two hundred and fifty dollars in the bank and no job prospects to cover our amassing costs. The home was lost, our marriage was ending, and I had two young children who deserved a better role model than the one I had become. I had to take my children and go, but my car was the only thing I had left, and living in it was quickly becoming our most viable option. With all the pride I could muster and then swallow, I called my parents and asked for help. They offered us a room in their home, and my children and I went from a four-bedroom, three-bath, twenty-four hundred square-foot house to a single room. The train crashed, and I hit rock bottom.

We packed the car and headed to my parents' house a state away. We uprooted the mess I had made of our lives and left the station. The train headed west, and in the rearview mirror, I watched as the house we made into a home shrank in the distance. Everything I prayed not to happen happened. Every fear that left me in the fetal position, begging God and the universe to prevent, was now my life. From this, I learned two things: first, when every fear you have is realized, there is nothing left to fear, and second, I could survive the realization of my worst fears. It ended an era of Devastation and Obliteration and began Restoration.

With almost no money, a bachelor's degree, and two young children, I decided it was time to take control of my path and operate the train myself. Depression, grief, and trauma had led the way long enough, and they weren't getting me anywhere. The problem was the tools I had on board could not sustain me. I had to learn who I was and what I could be. At thirty-seven years old, I had to give a voice to the twelve-year-old girl who had been stifled and buried in the ground with Jennifer all those years ago. I had to forgive myself for not knowing how to respond to that loss and making a great big mess of my life. I had to honor the friendship I had with Jennifer and celebrate the love we shared rather than sit in the sorrow of her death. I had to recognize that the light that once shone bright inside me was not extinguished on that fateful day. It was dimmed and reduced to a stifling ember struggling for oxygen. But it still burned, and I was the only person who could enflame it. That became my work. The work of a lifetime. But that kind of work takes time, and acknowledging a life of trauma response and defensive behaviors is only the beginning. I started Restoration simply and focused on tasks. I needed a job, I had to enroll my children in school, and we all needed therapists.

The train had been hanging off the rails for so long that moving an inch at a time felt normal. I had to break habits, which would take some time. The thought of that work made me angry. My anger made me fearful that I was not going to succeed. And my fear threatened to stop the train completely. But that was not a choice in which I could indulge. I was a single mother, and by rights, this was not earned by my two children. They deserved more. And so did I.

I took the first job I could find, earning a salary far below my skill level and gaining a two-hour commute. My time with my children dwindled, and I relied on my parents more than they could have ever expected when they offered us that room. I had no choice in the matter. I could not do it alone. I needed help. They provided it, and I accepted it.

The train was still struggling to make any progress, but fate worked in the background in ways I could not yet see. The position I earned was at a nonprofit agency. I directed a before-and after-school program serving impoverished children and their families. Here, I learned the value of service and the fruits of loving-kindness. I was earning very little money, but I was gaining knowledge, and I was helping others. I devoured the work. Everything about it thrilled me, from the families whose lives were improved by our services to the laws that governed our funding. I became curious about the nonprofit industry and fell in love with community service. My extracurricular activities were faithfully meeting with my therapist, naming my trauma, finally grieving the loss of my dear friend, and forgiving myself for being overcome with sadness.

I realized that immediately after her death, I cried endlessly for myself and the loss I endured. As I grew older, I cried for her and the abrupt and violent end of her potential. I grew older still, and I wept for the many people who lost her that day: her family, other friends, and an entire community. I recognized that her death caused so much suffering, and after all the lonely years of staggering down those tracks, I became aware that I had never been alone on that train.

As time passed, I finally forgave the man who ended her life. I accepted that no act is committed in a vacuum, and to become what he became took some doing. Whatever that was, I understood that he, too, had been a victim of something. Something powerful enough to make him kill, and that was a terrible fate. I saw Jennifer's death and the trauma that ensued in its entirety, honored the agony it created, and respected its power over me. But its reign over me was ending.

FINAL STOP: SALVATION STATION

After several years in my first nonprofit agency and the train seeking unchartered ground, I sailed headlong into a new dead end. My organization was going bankrupt, and changes had to be made. I was one of them. I recall the day our leaders announced the layoffs. A room of my peers was in desperate anguish as they mentally calculated their fate, the weeks or months they could survive without pay, and feared what would happen next. However, I quietly and inwardly smiled because I knew something they did not. I had already survived rock bottom, and I could do it again. I looked to the sky and breathed expectation into my heart. Whatever was coming was meant for me, and I embraced that not-knowing with hope.

As fate would have it, I earned a position at another agency, and my salary doubled. It was enough to afford a two-bedroom apartment. After three and a half years in my parents' home and decades of desperation before that, I finally gained enough physical and emotional strength to stand on my own. The light within me started to rekindle, and the train had a direction—Salvation.

I earned a master's in nonprofit leadership and management and continued serving the community. Eventually, I gathered enough knowledge to earn a position in federal oversight. My salary doubled once again, and I bought my first home entirely on my own. My children and I finally saw me as an independent woman, knowledgeable and successful in her own right. The rails beneath me stabilized, and I lived in blissful hope and faith.

I later earned a Doctoral Degree in Leadership, and upon graduation, I realized I had the personal, professional, and academic knowledge to promote widespread change and growth. The train I had traveled on all those years took me through dark tunnels and over vastly lit bridges, and I survived it all. I was courage and persistence personified, and I wanted to give that away. I researched the steps to starting a business. As a student of life, yet again, I immersed myself in everything I could learn about launching a Limited Liability Corporation, hiring an accountant, developing a product, and understanding the marketplace. After months of planning, I opened my own business. At fifty years old and thirty-eight years after that fateful moment that threw me off the rails, I was born again.

Among my many services to the community, I help people sift through the guilt, shame, blame, anger, and fear that block the path to inner harmony and peace. I share my story honestly. I do not deny the broken parts of me, and I characterize hope through a lived experience that includes despair and survival.

While nothing is perfect, and I have faced many setbacks, I have learned that fear, grief, and trauma are debilitating when left unchecked. When these feelings clog up your baggage compartment, you cannot help but run off the rails. There is no doubt that life can feel horribly unfair, but within those struggles, there are gifts. It took me decades to find them, but they became abundantly clear once I chose to seek them out. They became my blessings. Today, I see every struggle as an opportunity and believe I can handle anything that lands on my tracks.

All my past experiences show me that off the rails or not, I am all aboard.

ABOUT DR. DESIREE DEL-ZIO

Dr. Desiree Del-Zio is a proven management systems and operations leader with a successful track record of creating high-functioning teams. Her professional development is grounded in organizations serving children and families. Notable leadership roles include operations management, regional management, evaluation and monitoring, program design and improvement, and federal oversight. She earned a Master of Arts in Nonprofit Leadership and Management from the University of San Diego and an Education Doctorate in Organizational Change and Leadership from the University of Southern California. Dr. Del-Zio offers private consulting services, including Leadership Development, Executive Coaching, Strategic Planning, Self-Assessment Planning and Implementation, Gap Analysis and Organizational Change Management, Internal Monitoring Systems Design, and Federal Audit Preparation. In addition, she serves as a key contributor to the Early Intel Quality Improvement Network. Dr. Del-Zio and her fiancé live in Charlotte, NC. They travel the country helping nonprofits with guidance and kindness. She frequently visits her children; her oldest resides in Seattle, Washington with his boyfriend, and her youngest is completing a bachelor's degree in Asheville, North Carolina. As a family, they are Unstoppable.

Contact: *(760) 420-2874*
Email: *ddelzio1@gmail.com*
LinkedIn: *www.linkedin.com/in/desireedel-zio*

4

DR. DIANA KORAYIM

THE DAWN OF DISCONTENT

The sun's light gave me a perspective that three decades of unspoken animosity never did.

The sun peeked through the curtains. This day felt different. It illuminated the carpet in the bedroom I thought was the sanctuary of our love. I painfully pulled myself away from the warmth of the covers. I could not shake the weight of three decades of unspoken animosity between us and the suffocating grasp of a marriage that had long lost its luster.

The clock on the bedside table ticked loudly, a constant reminder of time passing as my husband slept unmoving on the other side of the bed. His snores filled the room like a dissonant symphony, contrasting sharply with the bitter thoughts that replayed in my mind.

"I'm tired of getting up early to go to work and care for the kids while you stay in bed," I blurted out, the words hanging thick in the air like a storm forming on the horizon. My spouse moved, muttering in protest as he tightened the covers around himself.

"You're always sick, always making excuses," I said, my irritation rising to the surface. "I've spent years working and raising our four boys practically on my own, and what do I get in return? Empty promises and broken dreams."

The room fell silent for a minute, as if the walls were absorbing the weight of my words and caving in around us. Finally, he looked at me with tired eyes, a mixture of indifference and irritation. "You know I've never been good at holding down a job," he whispered, his voice barely heard above the distant traffic. "I've got my reasons, and you should be grateful for what I do around here."

I tightened my hands, a combination of rage and frustration pouring through me. The lines of communication had long since been destroyed, leaving a vast space filled with the echoes of unmet promises. "I can't live like this anymore," I said, frightened but determined. "I need more than excuses. I need a partner, not a burden. The boys need a father, not an eternal child. It's time for a change."

As I exited the room, the door shut behind me, sealing in years of disappointment and paving the way for a path of self-discovery and recovery.

ECHOES OF PRIVILEGE

My roots led back to a childhood filled with ambition and love, where the perfume of success lingered in the New York air, blending with the salty breeze from the Atlantic.

My father, a great businessman with an affinity for real estate, had given us the comforts of which most people could only dream. Our spacious residence was a testimony to his prosperity, a home encircled by the gleaming façade of perfection. My mother, a socialite, had volunteered for the UN Women's Guild, navigating diplomacy with ambassadors' wives.

Growing up, our home was a rotating door of prominent person-alities, a gathering place for ideas that formed countries. However, I was raised in the shadow of honor, where success felt unavoidable, and the world was at my fingertips. Private Catholic schools, followed by an advanced university degree, portrayed a future destined for grandeur.

My two younger sisters personified the business spirit taught by our father. Their success tales echoed the theme of triumph over adversity. However, for me, the adventure took an unexpected turn.

Despite being accepted to Columbia University, an ivy-league university in New York, to study pre-medicine, the man who had promised to be my life companion opposed my objectives. I had a one-year-old at home, another on the way, a full-time job at a construction firm, and was going to attend evening school. It was a challenge I was willing to accept, demonstrating the same passion and ambition that had propelled my upbringing.

However, my husband's support remained elusive, hidden behind unsaid expectations. My father advocated for education, while my husband tied me to a life of seeming stability, suppressing my goals in the process. The ambitious young woman who once dreamed of medical advances found herself isolated at Columbia; her goals shattered like glass.

Devastation gripped my soul as the ivy-covered walls of academia faded into oblivion.

The route to self-discovery and freedom was impeded by the very person I had expected to be my committed advocate. Little did I realize the seeds of discontent planted in those times would grow into the thorns of a marriage based on broken promises and unmet potential.

For three decades, my marriage felt like a squandered chapter in my life. Despite the difficulties, there was a silver lining: four wonderful boys bestowed upon me by God. I enjoyed the responsibility of raising, loving, and admiring them. I remain endlessly proud and committed to their well-being until my death. My purpose focused on these boys, and I promised to utilize every ounce of my strength to support and assist them.

Unfortunately, my husband lacked the same level of determination. He remained mostly absent, allowing me to play the roles of mother, father, provider, soccer coach, chef, and homework assistant all in one. Faced with these challenges, my parents' unflinching support became my lifeline. They would drive from New York to New Jersey, showering me with dinners and offering to look after boys, especially my youngest boy for weeks at a time, giving me a small reprieve on weekdays. My mother's moving depiction of my youngest excitedly awaiting my return on Fridays, peeping through the open screen door, exemplified their level of involvement.

My father, a seasoned educator, had a significant impact on all my children's lives, particularly my youngest son's. Despite his youthful age of two, my father took him every place he would go—supermarkets and shopping stores—treating him like a young adult. His hard effort has clearly produced results, as evidenced by the excellent young man my son has become today.

As I think on those years, I understand that the importance of my role earned me the label of "Super Mom" by many. Looking back, I could never have done it all without the support of my incredible parents.

CACOPHONY OF DISCONTENT

The memories of our difficult marriage resound with the repetition of many disagreements. I remember yelling and screaming at my husband out of frustration.

"I'm not your mother!" I'd say, the words echoing throughout the house. "You're not my child!"

These desperate pleas became my rallying cry, escaping my lips until I was out of breath and red in the face. The internal rage I felt was like an enormous power and a silent storm threatening to consume me.

Our disagreements were frequently fueled by his refusal to accept the roles of father and husband, his financial carelessness, and his lack of love for me, his wife.

"Why can't you see what you're doing to us?" I'd beg, my voice heavy with years of anguish. "You never told me I was beautiful on our wedding day, and you still don't."

Even on our wedding day, he failed to acknowledge me—a gap that remained until the day I chose to disentangle myself from the web of our broken vows. I received compliments from others on my charm, character, and exotic features. But this was not enough for me. I felt I needed my husband's affirmation, which I never received.

His overblown self-image as a "pretty boy" proved ineffective, overshadowed by the fact that his charisma did not produce significant results.

"Your looks won't solve our problems," I'd reply, my tolerance fraying. "It's time to face reality and be a partner."

The story took an unexpected turn when he used my hard work, determination, and dedication against me, and yet still did nothing to contribute to the family.

"I've worked hard for this family, but you need to pull your weight," I'd say, my displeasure visible in my tone. "We can't thrive if it's a one-person effort."

RISING WITH ONE

We started to rise as family through my hard work and determination. However, this rise only scraped the surface of my father's excellent quality. I found myself juggling a delicate balance, attempting to maintain calm, composure, and some sort of order in the mayhem that became our life together.

In stark contrast to my quest of security through many professions, my husband's lack of desire revealed a harsh truth.

"Why aren't you looking for work?" I'd ask, exasperated in my voice. "We can't live on dreams alone."

The pressure to find work, keep it, or even consider working two or three jobs felt foreign to him. My efforts to support our family were received with a laissez-faire attitude on his part—a stark contrast to the commitment I put into every aspect of our lives.

His ease and nonchalance remained until he chose to stop working totally, citing the questionable excuse of very common symptoms most people have and he continued to search for medical reasons not to work. This frustrated me as this was his pattern.

"You need to find a solution, not an excuse," I'd say, with my exasperation at its peak. "People work through challenges, but you just quit."

While accepting that everyone experiences some type of bodily discomfort, the significant distinction was in the response. Many people persevered in the face of adversity, working despite their challenges. However, he took a different course, one that resulted in the entire suspension of his professional activities. The fabric of our marriage, which was already torn, continued to disintegrate at the seams due to his disinterest and excuses.

Throughout our difficult marriage, I anxiously tried to communicate my demands to my spouse. I grew up in a traditional home and acknowledge I had certain expectations of our lives together. During one of our arguments, I said: "I got married to have a man take care of me emotionally, mentally, physically, and financially." Unfortunately, these expectations were rarely fulfilled. The physical aspect, demonstrated by the existence of our four sons, was possibly the only proof of our promises. Nonetheless, calls for emotional, mental, physical and financial assistance which I asked for, and maybe begged for regularly, were rejected.

A PURPOSEFUL SHIFT IN FOCUS

The fact that my necessities remained unfilled brought me to a cross-road. Slowly, I gave up hope of finding these components in our relationship and made a conscious decision to shift my focus to my profession and children.

With an unshakable commitment, I pursued my professional development. I earned two master's degrees and a PhD from one of the most widely recognized universities in California, USA.

However, the verbal fights continued, a nightly pattern that felt never-ending.

I would confront my husband, expressing my frustration, "No woman would agree to continue like I have been doing with a man who does not support in any way whatsoever; no woman at all!"

It became a recurring refrain, "I'm the stupid one in this relationship to remain in this marriage."

The disparity between our contributions became obvious.

As I focused on my profession and schooling, the verbal fighting became more intense. I frequently found myself reinforcing the disparity of our partnership, a one-sided endeavor that left me emotionally, mentally, physically, and financially exhausted.

I kept thinking I would be the one to face premature death. I was burdened by the weight of an unfulfilling marriage and an absent partner.

Meanwhile, my spouse appeared unconcerned by the difficulties, basking in the ease of a life in which I provided everything—a free ticket to an apparently beautiful life.

The question remained: why would anyone change their life when they were provided for in this way? This internal conflict portrayed a complex picture of a marriage riddled with unmet expectations and the never-ending pursuit of a sense of accomplishment.

WHISPERS OF CHANGE

Amid the echoes of our turbulent history, the winds of change began to blow, bringing me to a crossroads that would redefine the course of my life. The option to relocate to Saudi Arabia appeared as a distant yet alluring appeal, promising a fresh start and the chance to break free from the shackles of a suffocating marriage.

As the decision loomed, I took comfort in the prospect of a new beginning. The notion of a life in a strange place, far from the battlefield of our linguistic disputes, seemed like a salve to my drained soul. The Kingdom of Saudi Arabia, with its rich cultural tapestry and promise of professional opportunities, presented itself as a canvas on which I could paint a different story.

The shift was a watershed moment, not only geographically but also emotionally. Leaving behind the familiar streets of our discontent, I set out on a voyage to a nation where traditions and customs told stories of history and change. Saudi Arabia, with its unique blend of modernity and culture, provided the backdrop for my transformation.

As the jet landed on unknown ground, the air was filled with a mix of excitement and fear. Riyadh's scenery, with its expansive desert and soaring minarets, reflected the immense expanse of options before me. This was more than just a move; it was an opportunity to rediscover myself, to unwind the threads of a life woven with unfulfilled aspirations and suppressed desires.

The relocation, however, was not without its hurdles. Navigating a new culture, conforming to societal standards, and adjusting to a completely different way of life presented challenges at every turn. However, within the maze of transformation, I discovered a strength within myself that had long been obscured by the shadows of my past existence.

The professional landscape in Saudi Arabia provided me with opportunity to immerse myself in a bright and dynamic atmosphere. Engaging with a varied population, I found peace in my job, which allowed me to express my passion and tenacity without the continual undertone of domestic strife.

As the days passed, and the weeks evolved into months, the unfamiliarity of my surroundings gave way to a sense of belonging. The desert breezes murmured stories of tenacity, and the minarets stood tall, testaments to the culture's durability.

The move to Saudi Arabia was more than just a change of scenery; it marked a transformative moment in my quest for personal development and fulfillment. In the middle of a foreign place, I discovered the strength to write my story, breaking free from the bonds of a past that no longer served me. The murmurs of change became a booming appeal to embrace the opportunities that lay ahead on this new voyage.

SHADOWS IN THE DESERT

The wide vistas of Saudi Arabia provided the backdrop for a chapter of my life marked by the flow of professional endeavors. The decision to relocate to the Kingdom with my husband and four boys under my sponsorship signaled the start of a journey that would reveal the complexity of our relationship.

In Saudi Arabia, I sought refuge in the organized regularity of academics, where the academic calendar provided the luxury of summers off, shorter workdays, and vacations that coincided with the boys' school breaks. It was a wonderful situation, allowing me to balance my job with the demands of raising four growing boys.

After eighteen years of embracing Saudi culture, my husband's condition remained unchanged. Despite intermittent efforts to find work, his inconsistent schedule and lack of career direction continued. The responsibility of being the primary breadwinner and driving force behind our family's financial security fell hard on me.

My children eventually returned to the United States to pursue their studies and personal growth. Two started at an all-boys boarding school in Connecticut, and all four finally returned to my parents in New York. The separation exacerbated the isolation in Saudi Arabia, where it was only my husband and me. His refusal to return to the United States and contribute to our family's well-being further strained our already delicate connection.

As I remained focused on my career, attempting to develop business connections and advance my professional status, conflicts at home grew. Late-night meetings and business negotiations became points of friction. My spouse, who was fixated on domesticity, despised my commitment to work, rejected the financial obligations that loomed over us.

The strain peaked when my husband returned to the United

States for medical reasons, but the only medical issue I saw were the challenges between us. However, his return simply increased my financial load, since he resided in my home without contributing to mortgage payments or acknowledging the financial hardship. His disregard for our financial obligations and hoarding tendencies increased the instability in our household.

Arguments became a daily habit, occupying six of the seven days of the week. The seventh day provided a small respite, a momentary silence from our ongoing battles. Despite several demands for divorce, my husband stubbornly refused, trapping me in a marriage that looked doomed to fail.

I grappled with the ludicrous concept that no man would accept a divorcee with four children, which spurred my decision to remain in an increasingly destructive relationship. The boys were my anchor, and their well-being was my top concern. Every day, I navigated the turbulence, hoping that the storm would ultimately pass and a semblance of tranquility would appear in the desert's shadows.

MY LIBERATION WAS UNVEILED

I spent the bulk of my life alone in Saudi Arabia, trapped by a commitment to a man with whom I no longer wanted to be married. The weight of the covenant pressed hard on my shoulders, legally tied, and restrained by the pledges made before God. Each night, my yearning to break away from the bonds of this union grew stronger. I continued to crave emotional, mental, physical, and financial security with no avail.

Attempts to reignite what had been lost proved ineffective. Thirty-one years of marriage marked a steady decline into a void, with occasional moments of enjoyment proving to be nothing more than flimsy facades—a simple cover-up to speed the passage of time. Despite numerous entreaties, the marriage appeared to deteriorate, plunging into an abyss with no hope of recovery.

In the shadows of 2022, a great awakening swept across my consciousness. A question struck me, "Why was I waiting for him to grant me a divorce?" As a US citizen and a woman with rights, I had the ability to recover my sovereignty. The choice to file for divorce, the result of thirty-one years of internal conflict, signaled that the moment for change had come.

My grown children witnessed the turbulent voyage. They had withstood the storms of our family relationships, even when they were young. But they did not understand the complexities. The choice to file for divorce, while clearly difficult, demonstrated an agreement that it was the appropriate option, long overdue.

The sands of time ultimately changed in October 2023, when the divorce was final in the United States legal courts. This monumental day, despite the intricacies of a divorce, provided an overpowering sense of freedom. It became the happiest moment of my life. It was like a ray of hope at the end of a long and difficult tunnel.

When I found out about my divorce, I felt a surge of relief and rejuvenation. The decision to end a thirty-one-year marriage, while fraught with grief for wasted time, provided unexpected independence and opportunities. Looking back, the one ringing affirmation that continued to come from this trauma were the four lovely and handsome boys I had the joy of raising.

The liberty was not limited to legal bonds; it also included my spirit and selfhood. The chapters that followed the divorce were characterized by a sense of rediscovery—a reclaiming of the lady who had spent decades in the background.

The scars of my past began to heal, and the prospect of a better future beckoned.

A NEW LOVE STORY UNFOLDS

In the wake of my divorce, a serendipitous encounter unfolded, introducing me to a man who would redefine the chapters of my life. It is a man I had never dared to imagine, one who saw the world through eyes that reflected boundless admiration for me. He is a man who, every morning, noon, and night, showers me with affirmations of beauty, and expresses his feelings in ways that resonates with my heart's deepest desires.

He is more than a partner; he is a revelation—a man who regards me as the singular presence in his life, a beacon of everlasting love. He is intelligent, handsome, kind, loving, caring, respectful, and a consummate professional. He hails from an elite family, exuding the refinement of a true diplomat. His actions mirror the red carpet he rolls out for me, a testament to his emotional depth and unwavering affection.

Every interaction with him affirms my belief that he was specially crafted for me by the hands of fate. He has become my true soulmate, my love, and the partner for which I had longed. Stability defines him, not just in his life but also in his career and personal affairs. To him, marriage isn't just a commitment; it is a testimony of love, trust, and honor for one another.

As the messages pour in daily, each one is a testament to his love and affection.

Our story unfolds like a modern Cinderella tale. He, my prince, and I, his princess, envision a future marked by unity and eternal togetherness.

To those who may see our union as a swift decision, I've always held steadfast to the belief that when you know, you know. And we are convinced that we are destined for one another.

Our connection surpasses the ordinary; we complete each other's sentences, share laughter that echoes into the future, and revel in the same joys. Disagreements, albeit slight, serve as catalysts for understanding, drawing us even closer.

He is undeniably my knight in shining armor, consistently assuring me, "I'm here to support you and take care of you."

In his embrace, I find a profound sense of comfort, safety, and belonging, feelings I longed for but never found in my marriage. He embodies the man I always sought, and with each passing day, our bond deepens. We look ahead, hopeful that our shared dreams unfold as planned.

This transformative chapter in my life stands as a testament that genuine love exists, and real men, true partners, are out there for every woman.

These are the lessons I've learned:

Do not settle.

Do not waste time on relationships that don't elevate and lift your spirit.

Life is short.

Make intentional choices that move you in the direction of your beautiful life.

Life happened, it hurt, we will heal, but more importantly, I learned who deserves a seat at my table and who will never sit at it again.

And my heart found solace in the arms of this extraordinary man, I discovered that true love is worth waiting for, and the promise of a brighter future is always within reach.

Now I always look forward to a new day, whether the sun shines or not.

ABOUT DR. DIANA KORAYIM

Dr. Diana Korayim, an American expatriate residing in Saudi Arabia, is an executive known for her exceptional leadership and dedication to excellence. As the Chair of the Women in Business (WIB) Committee at the American Chamber of Commerce in Riyadh, she fosters US-Saudi business relations. In addition, she has held roles as director, business development, and a faculty member where she drives transformative change, boosting revenues and market growth. With over a decade's expertise in data analysis, strategic planning, operations, project management, and construction management, she has handled multimillion-dollar projects excelling in business development and talent cultivation. She has co-authored a paper entitled *How Big Data Analysis Can Create Competitive Advantage in High Stake Decision Forecasting? The Mediating Role of Organizational Innovation.* Dr. Diana's impact extends beyond business as she actively supports societal progress, particularly in women's leadership, entrepreneurship, education, and innovation initiatives. Holding a doctorate in Executive Global Leadership from the University of Southern California, an MBA from the University of Massachusetts, and PMP certification, her credentials solidify her prowess in leadership, business, and project management. She is also a proud mother of four amazing boys.

5

DR. ELIZABETH WALKER

STIRRED, NOT SHAKEN

I WAS ALWAYS MY OWN STRENGTH BUT IT TOOK ME YEARS TO UNLEASH IT.

The most difficult experiences of my life float to the top like froth on a latte, waiting to be seen and acknowledged. These lessons underpin *who* I am, the ones that make me unique. They also color my decisions and contribute to how I see the world around me.

Connection, curiosity, and life-long learning... these are the values that make me tick. I seek out authentic connections with others and am insatiably curious about human decision-making, what motivates others, and how others make sense of the world around them. I am passionate about solving problems. I firmly believe that we can always do better and improve if we are open to possibilities and creativity.

Even though I am passionate about authentic connections with others, I don't like being vulnerable. Putting myself out there is definitely an uncomfortable space for me to live. Recently, I committed to practice authenticity and now realize that vulnerability and authenticity aren't always the most comfortable for people who aren't used to it. They're *frenemies* at best.

Today, however, I am willing to be vulnerable and put myself out there in hopes of sharing some of my greatest life lessons to be of service to someone else.

Throughout this chapter, I am sharing a couple of layers that contribute to who I am—a few of the painful, difficult, yucky experiences—because *these* experiences have proven to be my greatest teachers and how I have leveraged my strength and become who I am.

Staying vulnerable is a risk we have to take if we want to experience connection.

— BRENE' BROWN

ALWAYS A "GOOD GIRL"

7th Grade Year Culture Shock

I joined the tennis team at my public junior high. I wanted to meet other kids and this was a good way to do it. It was my first year at Ridgemont Junior High (I'd been in private school since kindergarten). Before starting school at Ridgemont, I saw myself as a mostly typical twelve-year-old girl of the 80s. By then, I was my current height of 5'8," had braces to straighten my eye teeth (aka "fangs"), and sported big hair (streaked subtly orange) due to repeated Sun-In applications.

Academically, my junior high years were a repeat of what I'd already learned in private school, so that part was easy. On the other hand, from a social standpoint, I was immediately immersed in a washing machine of dirty water for which I wasn't prepared. As a result, I spent the rest of junior high in a state of culture shock.

My typical week in Junior High:

- Mom takes me to school. I slink out of her Jaguar when dropped off, embarrassed and hoping no one sees me. If they see me, will *they* think that *I* think I am better than everyone else?
- I walk to my locker (or to class, lunch, gym, anywhere). Guys are on both sides of the hallway, leaning against the lockers, cat-calling, "girl, you so hot!" and "come on over here so I can ..." (you get the point). Hoping my heart doesn't beat out of my chest, I whisper to myself "don't look," "ignore them," "don't instigate them," "look confident," and "I won't let them get to me."
- Go home from school. Meet up with a couple of neighborhood friends to hang out until dinner. Go into the neighborhood woods, talk, and smoke cigarettes.
- On the weekends, find an older friend who drives to ride around town ("town" was three stoplights long), music

blaring out of the T-tops, singing at the top of our lungs, doing my best to hide my whereabouts from my parents, and trying my best not to get caught.

Mr. Campbell Traumatically Changed My Life

Now, back to tennis. One of my teachers, Mr. Campbell, was also the tennis coach. Mr. Campbell was young, just out of college, tall, dark hair, and married with a child on the way. Since he ignored most of the shenanigans that ensued in class and rightly presented as roughly thirty years younger than the next youngest teacher, the students classified him as the "cool" teacher of Ridgemont Junior High. All of the twelve-year-old girls had a crush on him, and the guys sat by and watched with jealous, piercing eyes.

I ended up taking tennis lessons from him over the summer. We generally played at the Ridgemont Country Club courts. One day, I called him to tell him that I couldn't make practice, because my parents were out of town enjoying a well-deserved vacation exploring the Great Wall of China. He offered me a ride to and from my lesson, and I enthusiastically accepted.

Instead of going to the usual Country Club, he said we were going to the Rich Park courts instead. His words lingered in my mind and then began rolling around in my gut like upset. Everyone always said not to go to Rich Park. It wasn't safe. Listening to my logical brain, I went along with it. What could possibly happen? He WAS my teacher, my coach, and was driving after all.

When we got there, it was noticeably quiet. No one was there. No one was *anywhere* that I could see. On top of that, the sun beat down on my unprotected fair skin, no sunscreen for me (this was the 80s after all), well over 100°F, humidity that could be cut with a knife. A typical summer day in the South. I felt exhausted from the heat and needed a break. Coach said we could sit down at the picnic tables over in the shade.

Coach started talking about his wife and baby to come. They met in college. He painted a picture of his college days as I constructed his college photo album in my mind. Lots of partying. Lots of drinking. I was shocked to hear these confessions from my teacher, no matter how young they were. Where I grew up, students and teachers just didn't talk about these kinds of things. My gut started talking to me again. Something was off.

My Assault and the Aftermath

Next thing I knew, Mr. Campbell was on top of me, kissing me, on the picnic table.

I pushed and kicked as hard as I could, and fortunately, was able to get away from him and run, as fast as I could, through Rich Park. "Get in the car," he said as he pulled his car up beside me. "Get away from me!" I screamed, hoping and praying that someone would see us and intervene. No one did. "I'll take you home," he said. Over the course of a few seconds that felt like years, I found myself weighing my options: I could continue running through an area that I was not familiar with and thought to be dangerous, or I could get in the car with him (which was also dangerous).

I ended up getting in the car with him. With my hands clutching the door handle and hugging the passenger side door, I said, "touch me and I'm jumping." I imagined what would happen if I actually had to follow through with that promise. Should I try to roll when I hit the pavement? I'd never been taught what to do in this type of situation. This was uncharted territory.

Luckily, he did take me home. Reflecting back, this story, *my* story, could've taken so many turns, and I was "lucky" for that day to have ended the way it did.

The emotional roller coaster that ensued was horrific though I didn't realize it at the time. Taking it one moment at a time, I planned for every possible contingency. What if *this* or what if *that*? I had to face him again next year at school. I'd be in his class. What would I tell my parents about not taking tennis lessons for the rest of the summer. The only thing that I was definitive about was that I would not tell even though my internal dialogue went something like this...

> OH, MY GOD! Did this really happen??
>
> I can't tell anyone about this. No one will believe me. They'll think I'm a whore (remember, I'm a "good girl").
>
> I can't BELIEVE this is happening. Is this REALLY happening?
>
> If anyone finds out, they'll blame me. Everyone thinks Mr. Campbell hung the moon. They'll never believe me. Would my mom even believe me?
>
> I can't believe this happened. Everyone LOVES Mr. Campbell. I can't believe HE did this. Did this REALLY happen or did I make it up?
>
> If his wife finds out, they might get divorced, and it'll be my fault and people will find out.
>
> Maybe I caused this because of what I was wearing.
>
> I CAN'T BELIEVE THIS HAPPENED!

Back then, there were no cell phones, social media, internet, no campaigns that brought attention to assault. I didn't know what *assault* meant. I was only told not to talk to strangers (and always abided by this rule), and Mr. Campbell wasn't a stranger. I *was* taught to be a good girl—which *really* meant to not sleep around, not dress provocatively, always say "yes ma'am" or "no sir," and always respect adults, especially teachers. I felt completely alone, unaware of the gravity of the trauma, how it would impact my sense of security and sense of self for years to come.

So... I pushed it down. WAY down. I was terrified. I had to face him all next year, AND he would be one of my teachers again. I'm going to *have to* interact with him.

I came up with a plan. I would ignore him the best I could. If I had to talk to him, I would do so with a pissed-off attitude—kind of like..."don't tempt me or I'll tell." I'm sure he knew I wouldn't. *I* knew I wouldn't.

Things Went From Bad to Worse with Mr. Campbell

Summer ended and eighth grade started. One day in Mr. Campbell's class, I passed a note to a friend, and Mr. Campbell made me stay after class. After the room cleared, he took me into the hall, "face the wall and put your hands on it. Spread your legs wide."

He paddled me on my ass in front of everyone in the hallway.

Humiliation is the only word that comes close to expressing this experience for me. Further insult to injury took place a few weeks later. He "caught" me in yet another transgression that led to another paddling episode in the hallway. This should have solidified in my mind that this man was a child predator.

Instead, of course, since I was already traumatized, my only thoughts were again...

OMG. IS THIS REALLY HAPPENING???

Reflecting now, as an adult woman and mother of a daughter, I am sickened and horrified. I think of all the girls and women who have endured similar and much worse from others they knew, respected, and revered. Other family members, teachers, religious leaders. I was from a "good" family, prominent in the community, upper socioeconomic class, church-goers. My mom was even on the school board for heaven's sake. If this could happen to me, it could happen to anyone. I know that *now*.

Fast forward to my college years. *That* part of my life was behind me. I was six hours away from home, and most importantly, Mr. Campbell. I was living my best life. However, ever present and invisible to others was that 'just under the surface iceberg,' knawing at me to right the ship before catastrophe ensued. I felt ashamed that I wasn't strong enough to report Mr. Campbell. What if he did this to other girls? At the time, I was not conditioned to see Mr. Campbell as a predator. After all, he WAS a teacher, and he *appeared* to the world as a clean-cut, nice, married man. At the time, in my naïve, young-child brain, I had assumed he did what he did because he was attracted to me or maybe, I thought in my mind, I made him do it because of something I wore to tennis that day.

I know *now* Mr. Campbell was a predator and knew exactly what he was doing. He knew exactly how I would behave and that I wouldn't tell. I was a "good girl" after all. He knew he'd get away with it.

Turns out he was wrong. Turns out that my sophomore year of college changed *his* life.

Mr. Campbell's Day of Reckoning

"Elizabeth?" Mom said when I picked up the phone in my dorm room. "Hey," I responded. "You're never going to believe this," she said. "A previous student has accused Mr. Campbell of sexually assaulting her. Can you *believe* that?" I knew the accuser, Karen, and we had been in the same grade. I'm fairly certain that Karen did not play tennis, and I also knew that people talked about Karen sleeping around. "She must be making it up. You know, she doesn't have a good reputation," Mom spoke in a lower voice. "I can't imagine Mr. Campbell doing anything like this."

My heart sank. I felt sick. After all these years, it turned out that he actually WAS a predator. Was he grooming Karen the same time he was *coaching* me? I wondered how many girls he had assaulted over the years. I did NOT want to deal with this. I wanted to push it down even further and never speak of it again. Act like it never happened.

The thing is, I was older now, more mature, (somewhat) wiser. I also knew that no one would believe Karen. After all, she had a bad reputation and that was about the worst thing for a girl to have in Ridgemont. I also knew that people *would* believe me. I was a "good girl" from a prominent family in the community. This time, the nineteen-year-old me made a different decision. *I* had the power this time.

"Mom, he did the same thing to me years ago." *Silence...* (Note: By "same thing," I meant that he used his power to take advantage of me. I have no knowledge about what actually happened between Mr. Campbell and Karen.)

As a mom myself, I wonder now what was going through my mom's mind. Was she worried what others would think when they found out? Did she want to protect me from having to go through this and potentially being labeled as a girl with a bad reputation? I have no doubt that she had strongly supported Mr. Campbell to the School Board already, just like everyone else on the Board. How would she reconcile this when the truth was known that she didn't know about Mr. Campbell assaulting her own daughter?

After a long silence, she asked me to talk to the school's attorney, which happened to be my childhood best friend's father, Mr. Tim.

I made the six-hour trek home to meet with Mr. Tim in person. All the way home, I was horrified and literally sick in my stomach at what I had to do. During grade school, I spent almost every day hanging out with his daughter after all. What was he going to ask me? How much detail would I have to provide? I was so embarrassed.

I did it anyway. Mr. Tim sat there while I talked. He was very stoic, a big prominent man, looking down at his shoes now and again as I talked. As soon as I finished, he said, "thank you, Lizbeth," and that was it. I feel sure my mom gave him a heads up about what I would tell him. I got in my car and went back to school. I didn't want to know what would happen next. I didn't want to stay in that town. I felt such conflict—I didn't want Mr. Campbell to lose his job. What would his family do? Would everyone in town know that I reported him? Would Karen know that he did the same to me? What would his family say? Would they be mad at me? Did I just ruin his and his family's lives?

In the end, all I know is that he lost his job and had to leave town. I have no idea where he is now... but I feel peace knowing I told the truth, even if well after the fact, and that my decision may have prevented him from harming someone else. Mom and I never spoke of it again.

HOW LOSING MY JOB WAS ACTUALLY A GIFT

Getting Fired

Well, technically, I wasn't fired. I was RIF'd (*reduction in force* if you're unfamiliar with the term) due to organizational changes. "Because we're integrating teams, there is some overlap in jobs. As a result, we're asking you to interview for your current job. Others can interview for it too," my new boss told me. What?? I'm interviewing for my *current job*, and others can interview for it too?? And someone else might be hired for my current job?? Am I hearing this right?

You see, I'd been successfully moving up the ladder since I started at the Fortune 100 company ten years ago. I had reimagined and reinvented the way we did business with our customers. My team had grown from about eight people to forty. We'd won industry-wide awards for our work, and I had personally won company-wide awards for my vision and leadership.

So, I played the game. I went through the process of interviewing for my job. No one knew it better than me, saw the future vision clearly, and knew exactly how to execute it. Turns out, I didn't get the opportunity.

My boss called and asked me to meet her. When I got to her office, she was on the phone, put her finger in the air, and mouthed to me, "I'll be just a minute."

So I waited, wondering what we were going to talk about. She stepped out of the office, smiling, "Elizabeth, come on in!" After apologizing for running late, she informed me that she was talking to another candidate that was interviewing for my job. "I've offered the job to another person," she informed me. "You know her, but I don't want to reveal who it is until she accepts. We're negotiating her compensation package now. Since she's currently in Sales, I had to find some extra money to be competitive with her offer."

Wow, I thought. My boss was essentially telling me that she'd offered my job to someone else, someone who did not have the appropriate experience, and she was offering her more money than I was making. *Is this even legal?* I wondered.

I was pissed, distraught, embarrassed, scared, and did I say "pissed"?? How could this happen? I'd always been successful at work. I'd worked my ass off for this company, traveled nights and weekends, rarely taking time off, all while being a single mom. I'd successfully grown my team from the ground up, rebranded and re-engineered our company's global medical educational platform and won numerous awards. How was this possible?

The truth is that it was one of the best gifts I've ever received. After I was transitioned out, a weight was lifted off my back. I was free to explore and create the next chapter of my life. In all fairness, I was burned out from all of the long hours and endless days of working at this company. It was never-ending, with few "thank-yous." I am certain that if I wasn't RIF'd, I would have continued to work at this company forever. I wouldn't have had the guts to quit given the company's stability and my compensation package. I would have missed out on the best job of my life.

Now, at the time, it certainly didn't feel like one of the best gifts of my life. I felt defeated, I questioned my leadership, and the ever-present "was I good enough?" was at its peak. But now as I look back, I am thankful for this key turning point in my life. It led me to identify the things that would be my north stars going forward: (1) have fun and (2) make a positive difference in people's lives. I have lived by that mantra ever since, and it has served me well.

Through my network and connections, my new role found me (even though I spent months in limbo), and it proved to be the highlight of my career (so far). I made life-long friends with influential people. I traveled around the world and was introduced to cultures that have changed my view on life. I was fulfilled with the work that was accomplished, and I had *so much fun*. I truly cannot imagine my life without this job, and I would have never had the experience had I not been "RIF'd," aka fired.

The greatest glory in living lies not in never failing, but in rising every time we fall.

— NELSON MANDELA

MY LIFE EXPERIENCES WERE MY GREATEST TEACHERS

Experience is the hardest kind of teacher. It gives you the test first and the lesson afterward.

— OSCAR WILDE

Every experience of one's life adds up to create the whole of a person, and I am a melting pot of all my experiences. Nothing happens by accident. It then becomes up to us to make sense of our experiences in this world and what we will do with that knowledge. Though my specific experiences have taken years for me to fully understand, I can't envision my life without them. They are a part of me just as watching my daughter take her first steps or watching her accept her high school diploma.

My life really began trying to make sense of trauma that I escaped. It found me. I had a choice to make at that point. My choice was intentional. This took strength, and so it began, whether I liked it or not, a path of me beginning to create for myself a series of unshakeable values and boundaries that served me well for the rest of my life.

Each experience colored my view of the world.

Some made me *cynical* and *untrusting* of others.

Some made me keenly *sharp* in reading others' intentions and *curious* about what makes others tick.

Some taught me how to *pivot*—just like a boxer dodging punches. Pivoting proved to be especially helpful during our long COVID lockdown.

Some taught me to be *resilient* and *agile* like being able to quickly devise a Plan B after Plan A goes to hell in a handbasket.

Some taught me *leadership*. Do the right thing even when that thing is really hard.

Some taught me about *power*—knowing when I have power to influence others and knowing when to use it to help others, standing up for others even when it means putting myself at risk, the significance of protecting, mentoring, and coaching others.

Some taught me *empathy* and *grace*. We never know what others are going through or what they have endured. My ex-mother-in-law taught me about empathy and grace during a difficult divorce from her son.

Some taught me about how loss can free us up for *exploration*. Having nothing to lose removes barriers and opens a world of possibilities. A sense of desperation can lead to *freedom*.

Some taught me about *strength* and never giving up or giving in. The strong women in my life (my mom, my daughter, my sister, my tribe) continue to teach me, inspire me, and show up for me *every.single.time*, no matter what.

Ultimately, my experiences taught me about my *values*, what I hold most dear, the true essence of my being.

Embrace your experiences, all of them.

Be curious and explore. Meet new people and connect with them. Share your stories—the *W*s and especially, the *L*s. Learn from other people and their lived experiences.

Nothing happens by accident, just like you are reading my story right now. If you want your life to change, you have the power to change it.

Most of all, show up vulnerably, and authentically. Your experiences don't define you. *You* do. They are a lens through which you learn and grow, go up and down, twist and turn, and like the froth of a latte, drink them all down, with insatiable thirst.

Remember, *you* are your own strength. It just may be time to unleash it.

Names and locations have been changed to protect individuals.

ABOUT DR. ELIZABETH WALKER

Dr. Elizabeth Walker, who goes by Elizabeth, is a life-long learner and self-described "unicorn" due to her wide-range experience. She is passionate about creating innovative and insightful organizational strategies that demonstrate impact. She is a clinician as well as global leader in marketing, market development, and learning and development. Elizabeth's leadership experience spans non-profits, Fortune 100 MedTech companies, and start-ups in the healthcare arena. She earned her Doctor of Education (Ed.D.) in Organizational Change and Leadership from the University of Southern California in Los Angeles, California. Her research focuses on women's leadership and advancement in the profession of spine surgery. Prior to this role, Elizabeth led the medical education team at the largest medical device company in the world, where she reinvented the medical education organization and won several *best in industry* awards with the development of mobile training facilities for healthcare professionals and the physician education platform. She also led the spine and craniomaxillofacial surgeon governance Boards and Committees at a global non-profit organization dedicated to advancing surgeon professional education.

Elizabeth remains focused on women's leadership and empowerment and helping organizations improve their business performance and outcomes.

LinkedIn: *www.linkedin.com/in/elizabeth-walker01*
Email: *mindshiftleadershipconsult.com*

6

ISA LARA MARIÉ

ON BECOMING A SHAMAN: THE GREATEST CHALLENGE AND HONOR OF MY LIFE

$\mathcal{N}$o one would ever want to be a Shaman if they truly understood it.

In the West, being a Shaman or a healer is often romanticized. However, it is a path of great challenge with many obstacles and constant initiation and near-death experiences. It is not something that a person chooses; instead, spirit chooses one to serve in this way. It is both a burden and an honor. It is full of trials, challenges, and service transmuting heavy energies on behalf of others. It hurts, it is painful, and it is exhausting. On the other hand, it is incredibly fulfilling, beautiful, and expansive, especially in connecting to the other realms. I would not trade it for anything because when I am doing the work of a Shaman, I am in my zone. I burn with passion and devotion to alleviate suffering. I am dedicated to supporting anyone and everything into healing. When I am doing the work of a Shaman, I learn more and more about the human and spirit connection and how I can best alleviate suffering. It is not a greater or lesser thing, nor is it something special; it is just a function that some people come in life to do. I happen to be one of many Shamans and here is my story.

MY JOURNEY TO BECOMING A SHAMAN

People are always asking me "how did you come to be a healer and a channel?" And they always phrase it as "what was your training?" All the experiences that happened to me in my life growing up served as my training, even more than a six-year apprenticeship I did with a mystic and Shaman in my early twenties. What I endured as a child, that level of relentless torture, abuse and darkness, was the greatest training I could have ever had and prepared me for the vocation of healer early in life. I wish I had known that I would become a healer, because I was lost and living in a kind of hell, and I was not sure if I was going to make it through for a very long time. I was what you call fractured, with very separated parts within my psyche. I consider myself one of the lucky ones. My core self stayed intact even though it went into hiding (called dissociation) for a long time. Many who endured what I did are not so lucky. I am also writing for them, that the energy through these words might touch or express for them that the pain and torture we endured as a group was not for nothing. *We are all connected.*

MY YOUTH SERVED AS THE BEST TRAINING FOR ME TO BECOME A HEALER

Training comes in many different forms, both formal and informal. I have had both, and many years of it, to become and excel in my role as a healer and Shaman. My best training came from my childhood. I endured years of torture, abuse, and neglect. I am currently writing a full-length book, due in Spring 2024, which will provide greater detail than I can here in this space. However, for the sake of brevity, I will detail some of it here so you can understand fully the journey on how it is I became a Shaman and how my purpose in life began at the young age of six years old.

MY FEELINGS OF NUMBNESS WERE A CLUE TO LATER DIG DEEPER INTO MY CHILDHOOD

Have you ever lived in a kind of fog like you were not quite there? Things are happening and you are watching but you are not connected to them somehow? During my youth I had fooled myself into thinking I was happy, or at least I acted happy. But deep within I was screaming, and I could not even hear my own screams. I had been taught to push everything down and tuck it away, any kind of truth or emotions in general.

When I was growing up, I always felt something was wrong, really wrong, but I could not quite put my finger on it. I knew some really bad things had happened to me and yet I was far away from it. I lived in this kind of floating, etheric space outside of my body, disconnected and dissociated. I looked happy and acted happy, because in my family anything other than that was taboo. Emotions were taboo. In the deep south where I grew up, I was taught not to cry and not express any emotions other than a smile. Everyone was so concerned with the image of how we looked in my family that how we felt did not really matter. I was expected, like everyone else, to push through and bear the pain and to be quite stoic.

I learned so well how to be stoic that I did not even know how I felt all those years. I was like a robot automatically doing what was expected. I knew what my mom wanted, what my dad wanted, and what the programmed Southern culture around me demanded. Yet I had no clue what I felt or wanted.

During my childhood and well into my twenties I played the part well. I had attempted to excel at everything I did. Maybe if I did the best job possible then perhaps somehow that would make me feel all right. I won the state tennis championship, was the Carousel Princess, top of my class, and loved by many. Yet, why did I feel so empty inside?

MY CORE FAMILY LIFE SERVED AS BOTH A BATTLEGROUND AND TRAINING GROUND

My family life served as one of my greatest training grounds to become the healer I am today. While I endured innumerable abusive experiences, they partly stemmed from two core people in my life: my mother and father. They were the conduits to serve me to the church for the ritual sexual abuse I endured, and later remembered. They were unknowingly delivering me to evil.

What I want people to understand, however, is that I do not blame my parents for this—I realize they were victims of their own family, ancestral, and generational trauma. I have spent years with therapists and healers to process and feel what I did not dare as a child and into my twenties. I was suppressed back then, but to fully heal and serve others now, I had to do this hard work.

MY PARENTS AGREED ON ONE THING: ABUSE AND CONTROL

My family life was more than challenging. Both of my parents were unavailable to me for different reasons, but they agreed on how to manage me as a parent: abuse and control.

My dad was an alcoholic, absent, collapsed, and unavailable. My mother was raging, cold and brittle. There was no solace at home and worse only was the abuse, punishment, and neglect. I was grateful that my physical needs were taken care of, but this certainly did not go past that level.

If I did what I was told and shut up, things would go a little easier. But it still did not stop my mother's outbursts of rage. Regardless of my actions or words, her uncontrollable episodes would ensue. She would blame, scream, and terrify me. She would come at me with threatening words and physical violence at times for some small act of spilling milk.

I had no father to go to for this as he was working in the day and drunk, unavailable in some other foreign dreamy world at night, or even passed out. They seemed to agree on one and only one thing: punish and control.

HOW I THOUGHT I COULD REGAIN CONTROL OF MY LIFE THROUGH MY EATING DISORDER

My inner world felt so out of control and my outer world ironically felt so controlled. I had no sense of self, of what I needed or even what I wanted. Into my teens it began to come out in an eating disorder. I started marathon exercising and starving myself for days at a time, eating merely an apple or some popcorn or morsel of food for several days or so until I could not take it any longer. Then I would have a normal size meal of whatever food I had been craving. By then my stomach had shrunk. I would often fall on the ground in abdominal spasms and terrible pain with my parents asking if I wanted to go to the hospital. I knew that I did not want to let my secret be found out. I would say "No, it'll be Ok" as I writhed in pain on the floor. This was repeated many times in secret, where my parents would not find me, and I certainly did not dare go to them for help.

It took some years before my parents caught on to what was happening as my weight lessened drastically and I became emaciated. My organs were extremely stressed and my moon time as a young woman was ceasing. It was at this point that they realized something was dreadfully wrong. They threatened to put me in an in-patient hospital unit. As they took me to the in-patient hospital facility one day, upon seeing it, terror flooded my body. I was chilled to the bone with a feeling that I would be trapped. I immediately promised them that I would try to eat more if they would just not put me in this dreadful place of walls and locks and sterility. There was not much light and I dreaded not being outside freely. I could not imagine being left locked in this box and controlled more. It felt like my world was closing in on me and it seemed like the ultimate form of control.

So, I faked it and went underground and hid my eating habits even more. I ate just enough to put on a tiny bit of weight, so I was not emaciated any longer. Running was my solace, sometimes biking, and sometimes swimming in the summer. But running allowed me to escape in my mind into some far away safe place. When I ran, I felt free and I ran as far as I could, miles and miles every day to feel the sense of power and freedom and, of course, to keep my weight down. I felt powerful when I was running and when I was thin. I pushed my body to extremes with very little nourishment and sustenance. I was getting more and more desperate to keep everything inside of me down, some kind of secret that I did not know needed to be remembered. It was getting harder to do this and I was able to still secretly sort of fake my way through my last years of high school and into college.

HOW MY MOTHER'S REACTION TO BEING ASKED IF I WAS SEXUALLY ABUSED PIQUED MY CURIOSITY FURTHER

Throughout my childhood and into my teens, I noticed several triggers around sexual abuse. I knew I was trying to escape the darkness. I had not yet begun to research, this came later, but I knew enough about myself and my body to know that something was terribly wrong and hidden. Traumatic experiences, especially the ones I endured, often tuck themselves away in hiding to protect the one who endured it. There were several moments up until this point where it tried to come out: through my eating disorder, mania to excel at everything, desire to control, and to be perfect. But I remained unaware of these signs and only instinctively at this point would gesture toward the experience I had endured.

Right before entering college, I attempted to ask my mother about being sexually abused.

I walked into the kitchen where my mother was standing and out of my mouth came "Mom, have I ever been sexually abused?" Most mothers, I think, would have at least a reflective pause or even become gravely concerned if a child ever asked them that question. My mother, on the other hand, became angry and replied, yelling "Never say that in this house again. How dare you say that."

I shut down immediately and felt embarrassed and ashamed. It was curious to me that when everyone in my family was watching a show on television and there was some sort of sexual abuse or rape scene that I would quickly jump up from the space, leave, and become nauseous. I always felt like I was going to vomit. I exited every time into my room, and no one seemed to notice. The level of checked-outness in my family was immense. I put this aside for some time not really knowing where it had come from, but I still had this very odd feeling rising in me that something was trying to get out of me. This *something* had lived within me for a very long time. I quickly shoved it back down again. I had to go to university now and it was my chance to escape.

HOW I BEGAN TO DISCOVER MYSELF AND REGAIN CONTROL AT THE UNIVERSITY

It was such a freeing day when I realized it was time to go to the university. Leaving was a sense that somehow, I had escaped my death and that I just might survive. I began to do what I wanted and explore things very different from my southern conservative Christian upbringing. I tried different forms of drugs and alcohol and became a bona fide hippie running around naked at times and barefoot. I allowed myself to get curious about what I was interested in for the first time. I had fulfilled my father's last request by going to the only university where he would pay for me. I was grateful to have that financial support and it was the last time he made a decision for me.

I began to get curious about myself wondering who this person was inside of me and how I allowed what was in me to come forth. I wondered what I really felt. I found myself putting posters of emaciated Ethiopian children on my college wall. Other people had sexy posters of models and musicians and here I was with starving people surrounding me. People would come in and ask me what this was about, and I would say that I never wanted to lose sight of everything else happening in the world. I wanted to remember and know about other people's suffering and stay connected to see what I could do to help. I wanted to remember to appreciate what I had and that I was lucky and blessed because there were many people who were suffering in the world who had been through so much more.

I lived with two psychotherapists at the time in a big hippie house. They were college professors on my campus and the husband would come into my room regularly and tear my starving posters off the wall. He would say "You're being a martyr. Stop suffering." I would then say "That's not what I'm doing. I'm here to remember so that I can help." In my slight, fairy-like eighteen-year-old essence I would then rise and put all those posters back on the wall and stand up to this tall, thin, wiry, wild-haired intimidating man who claimed he knew everything that was going on, especially inside of other people.

Once I went to the university it was like I could not stop running. I needed to get further away. I applied my freshman year to move to Italy for a semester to study Italian. I then took summer jobs in the American West for the national parks in remote high country wilderness areas. It was a time of freedom for me but at the same time I was still running from something, and I was not quite sure what that was yet. I found out later I was running from myself. Being out in the wilderness in the summers renewed my connection with God or what I call Source.

This was the first sense of peace I was experiencing in this place and a sense of renewal. Yet I still was not here and there was some faint feeling that I was not present. But where was I? It felt like I was constantly distant or detached from what was happening in front of me and that I was floating and emotionally numb.

HOW MY UNDIAGNOSED CHRONIC MEDICAL CONDITION
PROVIDED ME WITH MY GREATEST EPIPHANY

During the last season working out West for the national parks, I began to experience very deep pain in my lower back in the sacrum area. It was a slow deep ache and a pain that started to constantly move down my leg. The crew boss recommended I go out for treatment. I hiked solo the twenty-six miles on the remote trail from the middle of nowhere back to the nearest dirt road so I could get to the forest service station. From there I got a ride into town, which was Fresno, California. They could have medivacked me in the helicopter, but I was so used to pushing pain down that I chose to hike out. I certainly did not want to bother anyone or put anyone out.

In Fresno I saw a doctor. They prescribed physical therapy and anti-inflammatories. I did all the protocols even longer than the allotted time, but this pain was deeper, and it was not going away anytime soon. Later it would become my greatest teacher in this life.

I was able to finish that season on desk duty so I could rest my back. By then I had already finished my last semester and graduated from the university. But this pain, this deep aching pain in my buttocks, back and leg was not letting up. I began the slow arduous journey of seeing doctor after doctor and traveling across the United States, from North Carolina to California to see specialists. I had every kind of test you can imagine done at the hospital on my spine; cortisone shots, discograms, MRI's, bone scans, x-rays, everything the medical community delivered I would try. It either had no effect or I got worse from these individual treatments. All the tests were inconclusive, and the doctors were baffled as to what was causing this pain. I tried chiropractors, massage therapists, homeopaths, acupuncturists, and everything imaginable. I also did yoga, pilates, lasers, the list goes on and on. I even got my tailbone adjusted from within, which was unimaginably painful.

This went on for several years. By this time, I had become disabled and could barely sit for short periods of time. I could lift merely a coffee cup and nothing more. Any other weight would send shooting pain down my leg and into my sacrum. This was the beginning of rock-bottom. I was depressed, scared, and alone. I had become quite estranged from my family since escaping and was realizing the toxicity in our home. I was slowly awakening by the mirror awareness that I did not want to be there ever again. When I did communicate with my family and reach out, there was no support for me. My father claimed the back pain was in my head and my mother ignored me. I was on my own. I realized that I was an orphan and I had always felt that way. There was some relief in naming this and realizing it was the truth. Once I came to that realization, I had a breakthrough that changed my life forever: "I need to heal myself. I am going to heal myself. I don't know how but I am going to." At that moment I decided to learn everything I could about the musculoskeletal structure of the body. My partner and I packed up the truck with me lying down in the back and traveled all the way across the country to Seattle, Washington. I had met him while working in the Superstition Wilderness in Arizona and our love of nature bonded us. He was going to embark on his career with a wooden sailboat building business and I was going, by some grace of God, to see if I could enter massage school even though I could not really sit or lift anything. I could stand and lie down for some periods of time.

Thank goodness the National Park Service granted me with disability, so I was receiving some financial support. I tried many times to get help from my family in different ways, sometimes financially, as my father had a lot of money. But tiny snippets would be offered to me with great shame and blame. The message was given to me always that the back pain was just in my head and that somehow, I was making it up. My father thought I was trying to get his money or somehow just be given a handout. It was ironic because that is the opposite of who I am and my personality. I reflected on this deeply. I thought had I not demonstrated my achievements to you by over-excelling and overachieving in high school and college and doing my best by working so hard in multiple jobs? But I realized nothing I could do was going to convince my father otherwise, and that ultimately, I could not meet his standards of perfection. So, I gratefully received the tiny amounts of shame that he would hand to me in paper thin green colored pieces we call money. It hurt a little more every time and after a very short time I could not tolerate it. So, I stopped asking. And I went bankrupt from medical bills.

I could not go for walks or exercise. I felt so deeply trapped. I could mostly only lie down for long periods of time with short bouts of sitting and standing and walking short distances. I was not able to exercise any longer, which had always been my outlet. The darkness began to consume me, and the feelings started to boil and bubble. I was becoming increasingly uncomfortable emotionally and I was massively hurting in physical pain. No one seemed to be able to help me and Frida Kahlo became my hero.

So began my descent into massive depression, suicidal ideation, and into feeling completely and totally isolated. I thought endlessly about how to escape my body and how could I end my life or get out, but something in me could not do it.

After being in Seattle for some time, the pain was unbearable. It was rare that I could get relief even through some form of anti-inflammatory or muscle relaxer and my body was reacting to pain medication. I found out that I was allergic to opioids and codeine and was having trouble finding other options that worked for my body. I wanted to die so badly and leave my body and escape the sensations that never seemed to end. But something kept me going. There was some light that was directing me like a hope that was whispering to me and telling me to keep going forward and trust that I would find "the medicine" of what I needed.

Then one grace-filled day I met a man in Seattle in a bookstore who became a dear friend for many years. He said he knew a woman who was a channel and healer in the Seattle area, and he knew that he needed for us to meet. By this time, I was twenty-two years old and had been with this pain for three years, immobilized. I felt I had lost, in a lot of ways, the youth of my life. Channeling was not something I had heard of or experienced, as I was from a very conservative fundamentalist Christian background. Even so, I was very open to new things and exploring and I was curious. I was happy to give this a chance.

So, on a fateful day in the fall of Seattle I entered the home of Leta Rose.

This meeting forever changed my life. I woke up to the fact that I had been ritually sexually abused my entire life in the church. Horrific memories ensued and I embarked on a six-year apprenticeship with Leta Rose to become the healer I am today. I will share this story in full detail in my upcoming solo book *First Light*, which will be released in Spring 2024. Working with Leta Rose began my healing journey of reclaiming myself and healing my body.

WHILE HEALING MYSELF I FOUND MY PURPOSE AS A SHAMAN

I healed myself by working with Leta Rose and found my purpose in life as a healer and a Shaman. I have been doing this work for the past thirty-two years. I work as a medium, channel, energy medicine healer, and body-centered counselor.

My work is to be a bridge for people between the spirit realm and this realm. There is vast information and wisdom that comes from within each of our beings and I teach people how to listen to and access it. It is my life's work now, and my passion is to teach other people how to access their intuition, knowing, own inherent language of light skills, energy medicine, and channeling ability. This is not some kind of New Age woo woo application but very grounded evidence-based spiritual techniques of which everyone is inherently capable. Throughout my own journey of healing, I spent tens of thousands of hours studying psychotherapy, trauma, energy medicine, shamanic techniques, channeling, mediumship, the mind-body connection, and how to heal oneself. I combine my knowledge and expertise in all these realms.

I am excited to help others apply these inherent healing skills. Everyone has these abilities. It is not something magical or phenomenal. Sometimes these tools just need to be taught and practiced. I want to empower others with the ability to heal themselves and to help each other.

I see private clients remotely and in person. I also do group transmissions for people bringing in different frequencies of healing energies which I call Prayer Field Healing groups. I teach energy medicine to individuals and groups. I help people remember the chakra and vast energy system and the language of light of where we are all from; before we incarnate in a body as pure energy and consciousness. I teach ancient shamanic practices to help people remember how to become aware of their light body, otherwise called the aura. This includes how to maintain, cleanse the light body, gather, retain, and discern energy loss.

Mostly, I love assisting others in becoming more aware of and orienting as spirit in a body, remembering their true inherent nature and how to recover their energy from "the world," the place of habitual programming. This includes helping others to bring back parts of themselves that have gone into hiding. I also help others heal from all forms of trauma. I am dedicated to assist in "remembering" how to re assemble and bring back together disconnected incoherent parts of self into coherence. I also help people shift their attention to the inner space within so that they can attend to and see what is here and have more peace. My goal in life is to help people fulfill their dreams and destiny.

As a seer, I look to see what is in someone's Lightbody and being and what they are carrying. Then I simply move energy and bridge wisdom from the spirit realm to help a person access more balance and well-being. Mostly I sit with others in compassion, listening, and presence and allow what really wants to come forth to be seen, felt, heard and cared for with great nourishment. Sometimes all we need is a grounded loving presence—for Grace to come.

I write this story for you. I wish to inspire and encourage you to never give up and to know your inherent light and worth. I want you to remember that support is always here for you. Even when you're not sure where or how, simply go into the heart and ask sincerely for Grace to come, and mountains will be moved. Who you are is unique and no one else has those qualities or gifts you are here specifically to bring. You can access the vastness of your being. Know there is more strength in you than is imaginable. You are not alone. You are Unstoppable!

ABOUT ISA LARA MARIE

Isa Lara Marié is the founder and ordained minister of Eternal Grace Ministry, dedicated to the healing and awakening of all. She has served as a channel and healer in service to All That Is for over 32 years. Isa offers energy medicine/shamanic work, channeling, mediumship, and body-centered counseling. Her training includes 27 years of studying with a mystic and shaman as well as Hakomi certification from founder Ron Kurtz, and many other body-centered healing modalities. Her work is a blend of the Toltec shamanic lineage, along with angelic/galactic guidance. Isa offers in-person, as well as remote healing sessions and teaches energy medicine/shamanic trainings and prayer field healing groups.

Website: www.isalaramarie.com
Facebook: www.facebook.com/IsaLaraMarie
LinkedIn: www.linkedin.com/in/isa-lara-marie-
    4b58a1134
Instagram: www.instagram.com/isalaramarie

7

DR. JANINE LEE

LIFE IS LIMITLESS

*T*he only limits you have are the ones you place on yourself.

I am an Asian American, near-death experience survivor, recovered heart surgery patient, martial arts black belt, hopeless romantic who has gone on over 500 first dates, world traveler of 100+ countries, content creator, Certified Executive Coach, woman of color in technology, global learning and development leader, diversity equity inclusion champion, adjunct professor, keynote speaker, award-winning nonprofit founder, CEO, and author.

KUNG FU WAS INSTRUMENTAL IN SHAPING MY FIRST IDENTITY AS AN ASIAN AMERICAN AND MARTIAL ARTIST

I was born and raised in Oakland, California, in the 1980s as an "ABC," American-born Chinese. My father emigrated from Hong Kong, and my mother emigrated from Macau with their hardworking families to fulfill the American Dream. I was taught to follow the rules, be respectful to elders, do well in school, and be a *good girl*. To my classmates, I didn't want to be "too Asian," or I'd be characterized as a "FOB," a derogatory term for "Fresh off the Boat." I wanted to embrace my culture and my traditions, but I also thought it was *cooler* to be American. Juggling my dual identity of being both Asian and Chinese was always a challenge.

Growing up in Oakland, I lived on the border of East Oakland. I didn't live in the ghetto, but I knew where it was and what it was like. I'd visit my friends in neighborhoods with speed bumps on every street, shoes hanging from shoestrings flung across electric wires, black gating across house windows, and high barbed wire fences surrounding homes. This was pretty standard for the neighboring areas.

I remember feeling othered every time someone asked me where I lived. Comments such as "Why would you live there?" "Oakland is so dangerous; I'd never go there." "Do you sell drugs?" were common. I was embarrassed to tell anyone where I lived for that reason. Everyone had such a negative impression of Oakland and what was happening in my city.

From kindergarten to twelfth grade, I was sent to a small private school called Chinese Christian School (CCS) in San Leandro. I grew up in a homogenous environment surrounded by 99% Asians, sheltered from the rest of the world. A school bus would pick me up daily, drop me off inside our school gates, and take me back home. We learned Chinese, had Bible studies, and wore the blandest white shirt and gray skirt uniform.

I was introverted, shy, unpopular, and still finding my voice. My schoolmates would mispronounce my name on the bus as "Jeannie," "Jenny," or "Janice," and I didn't even have the courage to correct them. For a long time, I just let everyone call me whatever they wanted to. I had no idea who I was or who I wanted to be. One day, I was in San Francisco when a little Caucasian girl, no more than five years old, said to her mother, "Look Asians!" and pulled her eyelid to make her eyes look small. I was appalled that racism was happening at such a young age.

Although I always tried not to be "too Asian," I loved watching

Kung Fu movies with my family. I especially loved seeing inspiring women like Michelle Yeoh on the screen. One day, I walked by a Kung Fu studio in Oakland Chinatown and was in awe seeing my future Sifu practicing with a sword. "I want to sign up," I told my parents immediately.

Taking Kung Fu classes was one of my passions that changed my life. I had to shout when I was punching, speak up during practice, acknowledge my Sifu, and practice group forms. After throwing a 200-pound man over, I realized I was beginning to build my self-confidence and find my voice.

I didn't realize until I graduated why my parents wanted me to go to a private school. My parents valued a good education and worked hard as immigrants to send me to private school. The reality was that I was supposed to go to a high school down the street, Oakland High, with a 50% dropout rate, teenage pregnancy, gangs, and drugs.

When I started working retail in high school at GAP, Inc., it finally dawned on me that I lived a vastly different life. The colleagues I met were from different socioeconomic statuses. Some were single mothers providing for their families on a $7/hour paycheck. They struggled to make ends meet each day. I was grateful for the new perspective and wanted to learn more.

Throughout my childhood, these lessons stuck with me through my adult years:

1. I recognized how challenging it was to find my voice and get lost in the shuffle.
2. I understood what it felt like to juggle the dual identities of being American and Chinese.
3. I knew I lived a sheltered life and I was curious to learn more about other ethnicities, backgrounds, and lifestyles.
4. I was "othered" and understood what it felt like to be an outsider through growing up in Oakland and as an Asian American.

5. I learned how a passion such as Martial Arts could build my self-confidence and propel me forward.
6. I valued the importance of a good education and how it can shape your life.
7. I was grateful for the opportunities presented to me and wanted to pay it forward.

SURVIVING A NEAR-DEATH EXPERIENCE AT FOURTEEN YEARS OLD TRANSFORMED MY LIFE

While my adolescent years gave me powerful life lessons, there was one powerful moment that changed my life's trajectory: when I faced death. "This can't be happening," I said as I plunged deep into the Colorado River. I opened my eyes, and I saw a ceiling of water above me and almost pitch-black darkness.

It was in the ninth grade, and our class had taken a trip to the Grand Canyon on a river raft tour. I had fallen off the raft into the water and was struggling with my limited swimming experience to get back onto the boat. The raft came near several times with teachers and classmates trying to help pull me back onboard, only for me to hit my head and become entrapped under the raft several times without any oxygen. The waves were too choppy, my arms were giving out, and I was horrified to drown to death.

After a fight with the river, for what lasted over thirty minutes, I was pulled back on the boat. I could breathe again. I remember going to the emergency room, being told I was dehydrated and to drink more water. I couldn't stomach the water glass and felt like I was drowning all over again. I was terrified. I began thinking: What would I have accomplished in my life if I had died? I recognized I was just floating along metaphorically in life, an average B student, complacent about school, and with no legacy to leave behind. Although I had won the fight with the river, I battled insomnia and near-death nightmares for decades to come. I had a stark wake-up call to rethink life in its entirety.

ANOTHER BRUSH WITH DEATH MADE ME REALIZE I WAS CAPABLE OF ACHIEVING MORE

One day during Kung Fu practice, I felt light-headed and stopped in the middle of my routine. My Sifu asked me if I was okay. I woke up on the floor and was sweating. I had fainted. I started seeing a cardiologist because my heart rate would race every time I felt anxiety, stress, or adrenaline in my body.

The palpitations got worse and worse, happening several times a day, and impacted my studies. I started wearing a large electrocardiography (EKG) heart monitor for high school, work, and physical activities. My cardiologist diagnosed me shortly thereafter with supraventricular tachycardia (SVT).

My heart rate would abnormally accelerate to 250 beats per minute because of an extra pathway in my heart. Because it was happening so frequently, she recommended I take the next step to have an ablation heart procedure. I was only seventeen years old.

The ablation required the cardiologist to find the extra pathway in my heart and destroy it while I was sedated. As with all medical procedures, there is a risk you face, and my fear of death came roaring back again. I was scared that I might not even make it to college.

During the procedure, I remember a countdown clock, 3, 2, 1, and a stinging burn inside my chest. I woke up to hear the procedure was successful but immediately started crying when I realized I was sitting in a large pile of blood, the white hospital sheets drenched. Although this was supposed to be an outpatient surgery, the doctor requested to keep me for overnight observation and recovery.

When I woke up the next day, I decided I was ready to take on the world. I was still alive.

MY PURSUIT OF A LIFE-LONG PARTNER AS A HOPELESS ROMANTIC RESULTED IN OVER 500 FIRST DATES

When I was at home, my favorite pastime was watching romantic movies such as The Notebook, Serendipity, or 50 First Dates. I was a hopeless romantic. I would always daydream about finding the man with whom I would spend the rest of my life. I always knew I wanted to get married and find a life partner.

Growing up in a Chinese family, every family gathering was "Do you have a boyfriend yet?" "When are you getting married?" Although I wanted marriage for myself, I also felt familial and societal pressures to find a husband.

Dating never came easy for me. I read every dating book, followed the top dating coaches, and tried to get out there as much as I could to meet someone. I went on every single dating application, from Yahoo personals during my college years to recent ones such as Bumble, Coffee Meets Bagel, and Hinge. My online dating apps became like a stock portfolio I had to manage. I even tried speed dating; my record for the most dates in a week was about twenty-five.

My friends would find entertainment and humor in my first-date stories. There was the teacher who asked me to pay for the check because I ordered a $10 macaroni and cheese, which was above his budget. I also had to end a first date early because an ex-girlfriend was stalking my date and on her way. Of course, I also got catfished several times with men who did not look like their photos. I met some really interesting people but also felt discouraged after every date.

If my near-death experiences had taught me anything, it was not to give up because life is too short. There was someone out there for me, and I knew I had to find him. Anything worth having is worth working hard for, so I dedicated time to going out on several dates a week.

At some point, I realized that I was intimidating other men

because I was perhaps too successful in my career. Friends started coaching me to "dumb it down" or "don't talk about work." But I really just wanted to be myself and not hide my successes.

My mother would tell me that she believed there wasn't just one person out there for me but multiple people with whom I could be compatible. During our trip to Thailand, I remember feeling a huge burden being lifted off my shoulders when I asked her, "Would I let you down if I never got married?" and she responded "Absolutely not. That's up to you to decide. I just want you to be happy."

At the onset of the COVID-19 pandemic in March 2020, I was about to give up after having been on about 500+ first dates. "I'll never meet anyone at this rate." I reviewed my dating filters and adjusted some of my preferences. I thought it might be odd to date someone younger than my brother, who was three years younger than me, but I decided, why not go four years younger?

There he was, my future husband, Jordan. He popped up on my screen because he recently celebrated his birthday in February. Dating during precarious times like the pandemic, you really learn about another person. He didn't pressure me to go on a first date. We spent lots of time getting to know each other on the phone, watched Netflix movies on the phone together, developed an emotional connection, and eventually met for a walk with our masks and sunglasses for our first date just like an episode of "Love is Blind" where you can't see each other's faces.

When everything is on lockdown, you also fast-forward to what it would be like if it were just the two of you, enjoying each other's company, without anything else. The pandemic flew by with him by my side. We got engaged in 2021 and married in 2022. Jordan is truly the most amazing partner I could have ever dreamed of and more. He was never intimidated by me or my success. He saw us as a team.

In my 20+ years of dating, I learned that I had to love myself first before someone else could love me. The self-confidence I built eventually attracted my future partner. I also became crystal clear on what I was seeking. I learned not to waste time by getting distracted by men who would compromise my non-negotiables.

The best dating advice I received was to make a list, divide it into three columns, and write down my must-haves, nice-to-haves, and deal-breakers. This rigorous exercise taught me what I really wanted in a partner. I see more clearly now how I could have cut through the "noise."

Many things I was looking for in a partner, such as age, didn't really matter at the end of the day. What mattered most was that someone would love me for who I am, especially during a global pandemic, where what you get is me and all of me. I found someone who was confident in themselves and who would complement me. As time-consuming as the 500+ dates were, it was all worth it in the end when I found my husband. Resilience isn't just about life failures and your career; it's also about love and relationships.

WHAT TRAVELING TO A HUNDRED COUNTRIES TAUGHT ME ABOUT CULTURE, GRATITUDE, AND MYSELF

My mother tells me my first international trip was as a child on a cruise to Ensenada, Mexico. However, it wasn't until after I graduated college and went to Japan and Hong Kong that the travel bug really bit me. My family also loved to travel, and every year, my brother, my parents, and I would take an annual family trip together. I'm so blessed to have traveled to six continents with my family.

My most memorable trip was my first time in Africa, when I went on a safari in Kenya and Tanzania. I remember the first few lodges having running water, electricity, and heaters. By the time we reached the end of the trip, we were camping in the middle of nature. It was a stark reminder of what it would be like to live without the things we take for granted daily.

What really struck a chord with my heart was when I learned about the polygamy practiced in some of the Kenyan villages where men were allowed to marry up to four women. One of the other travelers asked our guide, "How is that possible? Is there a ratio of four women to every man?" The response we received was shocking; men would just marry younger and younger. We visited villages with sixty-year-old men who were marrying their fourth wife of fourteen years old.

Moreover, if the husband passes away, the woman will marry the next of kin, possibly a brother or uncle due to the dowry her family received. Essentially, the man's family owned the woman. Many women also faced domestic violence and physical abuse but could not leave their husbands because they would have nowhere to go. Our tour guide told us that there were some shelters to help women escape these circumstances but not enough support.

My heart was broken for these women. I remember sitting there that evening crying, thinking how can we live in a world where women are treated like this? My mind was racing thinking about what life would be like if I weren't born in the United States. I lived in a completely different world, and the trip to Africa gave me a new perspective and gratitude.

The following year I wanted to go back to Africa. During my MBA program, I was accepted into the Seminar in International Business (SIB) course in South Africa. My life-changing experience happened over the course of the week.

I remember walking through the Apartheid Museum and crying to see the violence and pain South Africans faced. "Why do we have a museum like this? It's just so heartbreaking and painful to see." I remember someone saying, "So that it never happens again." The experience heightened the need for my future leadership in DEIB and to be an advocate for racial equity.

When I came home, I felt reinvigorated as a newly born person. I aspired to be a Servant Leader like Nelson Mandela, my new role model. I fell in love with South Africa and told myself that whenever I travel somewhere again, I want to learn about a country's history, people, culture, food, and customs to immerse myself as I did in South Africa as a student.

As a learner, I always wanted to visit as many countries as possible because I knew it would broaden my perspective in life just as the two trips to Africa had. As I began my first global role in the technology industry, I was thrilled to have the opportunity to travel for work. I optimized my routes for business travel, my schedule, and my budget to make it happen.

I thoroughly planned visits to new countries with intentional layovers or "side trips" to nearby destinations I had never been to. For example, if I traveled to Belgium for business, I would fly to the Czech Republic the weekend before and to Hungary the weekend after. And thus, Jetset Janine was born.

Although I loved to travel, I often had to travel alone for work or my side trips. As someone who struggled with making friends growing up, the thought of eating alone at a restaurant or watching a movie at a theater by myself scared me. This was going to stretch me beyond my limits. As a solo female traveler, I had to learn to be comfortable in my own skin, to be alone with my thoughts, and to spend a lot of time on self-reflection.

I remember showing up at the airport in Zimbabwe alone, looking for my driver, and then spiraling into anxiety that I may have transferred money to a fraudulent bank account, and no one would be there to pick me up. I had to think on my feet, ask for help when I was comfortable, and be more intuitive of people's intentions. The trip to Zimbabwe ended up being an incredible experience where I made new friends all over the world, walked with the lions, and continued to build my self-confidence by initiating deep conversations with complete strangers.

I grew stronger and more independent and became more comfortable being alone. Instead of feeling isolated or alone, I felt empowered. This is why I highly recommend everyone travel alone outside of the country at least once in their lives. You will learn more about yourself than you ever imagined.

When you explore another country, I highly encourage you to do your research and read about its history, customs, and culture before you arrive. I love focusing on the experience, what you will learn from the people, where the locals go, where the hidden gems are, and how I can learn about the culture. I also encourage you to take notes, photos, and videos during your trip to relive the moment and reflect after you get home. What did you learn about the country, the world, and yourself? What new perspective has this country given you?

Over a hundred countries later, I can tell you that each country has taught me something about myself, who I am as a person, and who I am as a leader. I never worry anymore about who will come with me; instead, I am excited about who I will meet. I look forward to sharing more details about my travel adventures in a future book.

"GOING ALL IN" WITH MY LEGACY FOR SERVICE, LEADERSHIP, AND THE WORLD

My near-death experiences, coupled with my pursuit of the facets that matter most to me in life, have given me the fire to accomplish my pursuits in my heart and soul.

After my near-death experience, I took AP classes and became an A student. I was more social, put myself out there to make friends, and learned how to "be my authentic self." Shortly after completing my heart operation, I returned to training in Martial Arts as a recovering tachycardia patient and became physically stronger. My chest would hurt initially anytime I had adrenalin because it felt suggestive of the heart palpitations I experienced with my heart condition, but I got used to the discomfort, and eventually, I stopped being scared, and over the years, the discomfort went away.

At nineteen years old, I achieved my Black Belt in Kung Fu, was a local Grand Champion, and was a spokesmodel for Kung Fu Magazine. During college, I made lifelong friendships and was even the President of a sorority, Sigma Omicron Pi. I really stretched myself socially to grow my self-confidence, find my voice, and develop meaningful relationships.

At twenty-one years old, I founded a 100% volunteer-run nonprofit, Capture the Dream, Inc., based in Oakland, focused on making educational dreams come true for underserved youth in the Bay Area. My passion for education and fostering more equitable outcomes came to life. Since its inception, the organization has served over 4,000 individuals and distributed over $300,000 in goods and services through backpack school supply drives, providing educational field trips, mentors, scholarships, and other programming to remove educational inequities.

As a result of my leadership in community service, I received the Maybelline New York Empowerment through Education Award in 2006 and was featured in People Magazine's Heroes Among Us Issue. I also received dozens of other accolades, including a "Janine Lee Day" from the Mayor of Oakland and a Jefferson Award from Barack Obama.

As a young founder and CEO, I had to learn how to build a company with minimal work experience. I had to create a compelling mission and vision that would lead 100+ volunteers to make a positive impact in our communities. I learned how to motivate and inspire followership, make valuable networking connections, create programming for underserved youth, and build a company from scratch.

However, leading a community organization also had its challenges. Due to a misalignment in values and operational differences, I had to end a relationship with my previous non-profit mentor. I also stretched myself too thin and burned out a few times, ending up in the hospital. I struggled to find the financial support and resources to sustain the organization, and unfortunately, due to COVID, operations stagnated. Each challenge made me stronger and more resilient, and I am still hopeful that one day Capture the Dream, Inc. can find the full resourcing and support needed to carry forward into the future.

While running Capture the Dream, Inc., I juggled my corporate job as a Senior Manager at a Fortune 500 energy company. I led a team of twenty-five direct reports and got certified as a Lean Six

Sigma Master Black Belt, an expert in continuous improvement. While balancing the nonprofit and corporate job, I also graduated from the UC Berkeley Haas School of Business in the Evening and Weekend MBA program on a full-ride scholarship. Simultaneously, I continued my passion for Martial Arts, pivoting to Muay Thai kickboxing and maintaining a healthy lifestyle.

When I graduated with my MBA in 2014, I explored my next opportunity for growth. I received my certification as a Certified Executive Coach through the Berkeley Executive Coaching Institute, and I started teaching as an Assistant Lecturer for the Seminar in International Business (SIB) Program at UC Berkeley Haas' MBA program, the program that changed my life.

In 2017, I recognized I was ready to switch industries from energy to technology, an industry pivot I was told I had less than a 5% chance of achieving. To make this pivot, I took a step back from my ten-year career as a Senior Manager and transitioned to an individual contributor role. Seven years later, as a woman of color in technology, I'm proud to now be a Global Head of Learning and Development at a Fortune 500 technology company. I pursued a successful career while traveling to over hundred countries, creating content about my adventures, actively dating to meet my husband, training in Muay Thai, and starting my own executive coaching practice.

My growth mindset and desire to learn could not be dispelled. I returned to school for my final degree, my Doctorate in Education with an emphasis in Organizational Change Leadership at the University of Southern California while working full-time. In 2023, I published my dissertation on workplace belonging for women of color in technology. As a DEIB (diversity equity inclusion and belonging) expert, I've been invited to speak as a Keynote Speaker all across the nation in various forums, publishing articles, interviewing on podcasts, and coaching others.

My life mission is to inspire others to reach their full potential, and my life vision is to create a world where everyone belongs. I've aligned each of my identities to accomplish my mission and vision. I found my authentic voice, my meaning in life, and the opportunity to build our future leaders. Most importantly, I'm surrounded by love and happiness, and I wouldn't change my life. I am blessed to have my "village" of cheerleaders —an incredible husband, family, and lifelong friends who support my endeavors.

YOU ARE LIMITLESS

Life isn't easy. Reflecting on my early years, I started out lost in the shadows, a shy "B" student who didn't know who I was, who barely showed up, and who had no friends. I was just getting by and doing what was expected of me most of the time.

A series of challenging experiences jarred me into action when I realized any day could have been my last day on this earth. But even then, I had a choice to make. It was up to me to reflect on those experiences, make some intentional shifts in my life, and unlock what I was capable of. This drive and momentum have propelled me to accomplish many things in life; however, I am still finding the right balance so that I don't overextend myself or burn out.

"How do you do it all?" This is the number one question I always get. I chose to be intentional, pursue my goals and ambitions, set well-being boundaries, and leave my legacy. Whether you call me the Janine of all trades, the woman with multiple hats, the cat with nine lives, the Renaissance woman, or the modern-day Wonder Woman, I've lived multiple lives, careers, and identities in a short amount of time. I am Unstoppable.

What I've also realized is there is more to a person than meets the eye. You typically will only get to know one dimension or identity of someone you meet. I choose to always lead with compassion because you never know their past trauma, present challenges, or future potential. Nor do you know what hidden talents someone possesses by their resume alone. Your strengths and life experiences go beyond what is listed in your qualifications when you apply for a job.

Having danced with mortality a few times, I've realized you only live once, but you can create your life to be more than one thing. You don't have to fit into one box. You can have multiple identities, talents, professions, and passions. You can choose to be alive, limitless, and unapologetically yourself.

It's up to you to create the life you want and the legacy you want to leave. Recognize your life vision and be intentional. I challenge you to overcome the idea of having a singular identity and honor your multiple identities. Embrace the lived experiences that have shaped who you are today, and that will shape you tomorrow.

You are limitless!

Learn more about Dr. Janine Lee here:

ABOUT DR. JANINE LEE

Dr. Janine Lee is an award-winning Global Learning and Development (L&D) and Diversity Equity Inclusion and Belonging (DEIB) Leader with almost 20 years of experience at Fortune 500 companies. She is a certified Lean Six Sigma Master Black Belt and a UC Berkeley Haas Graduate and Certified Executive Coach. Janine has taught DEIB, leadership, communications, digital transformation, and international business at top universities, including UC Berkeley Haas School of Business, Santa Clara University, and UC Berkeley Center of Executive Education.

She is also a USC Doctor of Education (Ed.D.) graduate and has won dozens of local, national, and internationally acclaimed awards for her leadership such as the Maybelline New York Empowerment through Education Award, PG&E Diversity Champion Award, Bank of America Local Hero Award, L'Oréal Paris: Women of Worth Finalist, and Jefferson Awards for Public Service. She has also been featured in media such as People Magazine, KTVU News, Oakland Tribune, and the SF Chronicle. Born and raised in Oakland, California, Janine is a near-death survivor, keynote speaker, 100+ country world traveler, content creator, and martial arts black belt. Her life vision is to "create a world where everyone belongs," and her mission is to "inspire others to reach their full potential."

Website: *www.janinelee.com*
LinkedIn: *www.linkedin.com/in/janinelee*
Instagram: *www.instagram.com/drjaninelee*

8

DR. LILLY TAM

CAN I LIVE WITH YOU?

1978 LOS ANGELES, CALIFORNIA

*I*magine a young mom in her 20s with three kids under the age of six, her husband, and her mother-in-law living in a cramped, tiny one-bedroom apartment. Chaos often filled that apartment, but today would be the most memorable for everyone inside. The young mom's husband and mother-in-law locked themselves inside the bedroom with her three kids to get away from her. She can hear her kids crying. Her husband angrily shouts, "Go away! We don't want you around anymore!" The young mom keeps banging on the door and screams, "Those are my kids! Let me see them! Let me in!" Her mother-in-law responds by spitting at the door and shouting in Chinese, "Shame on you for the shame you bring to our family." This only aggravates the young mom more as she tries to kick down the door with all her strength while scream-ing, "What did I do wrong?"

Her husband ignores her and instead yells at their youngest daughter, who is barely three years old, to shoot at her mom's feet with her little toy water gun. Tears are running down her little face and she's so confused. She sees her mom's feet under the doorsill and presses the trigger again and again. Soon after, the police show up at the door. They take the mom away in handcuffs and put her in the police car. This family doesn't know it yet, but it will be the last time they will all be together under the same roof.

This was a scene from my childhood. I was the youngest daughter, shooting water at my mom's feet with my water gun. I replay this memory over and over in my head, like a scene from a movie, trying to make sense of what happened. I remember begging my mom for the water gun at the market the day before. We were very poor; we barely had enough money for food, yet she reluctantly bought it for me. But the next day, I was soaking her feet with it. I have carried so much regret and guilt over that moment. My mom must have felt so betrayed by me, and I never had the chance to apologize.

My parents immigrated to America as young adults. They never told me, but I assume it was to achieve the "American Dream"—the hope of living a better life. I am not sure if struggling to make ends meet in a cramped one-bedroom apartment in Los Angeles was what they had in mind. After my mom was taken away, she was diagnosed with schizophrenia and then placed in a mental institution. My father gave up his rights to custody, and we never heard from him again. From then on, we would start our journey into the foster care system.

SURVIVING FOSTER CARE

According to Chinese customs, my family's misfortune would result in us being considered outcasts, the unwanted, the unlucky. This is how we were treated by every foster family. Every time the social worker walked out the door, the foster families' demeanor would instantly shift from joyful to a look of pure repulsion and disgust as they laid eyes on us. They never had any intention of caring for us, anyway. Their only goal was to receive the government check for foster kids. Consequently, we moved from family to family often.

Our stays usually only lasted a few months. We would pack what little we had in a black trash bag, then wait to see where we were going next. It was difficult to place the three of us together, I was very young, and my big brother had special needs. Until one day, one foster family said "Yes!" to all three of us. They assured our social worker they were ready for three kids as they were empty nesters with just one teenage son left in the house. I was so excited. On our first visit, we all got so many compliments. They liked how quiet my brother was, not hyperactive like other boys. They thought I was so cute with all my questions, and they especially liked how my sister was pretty. I was also excited to meet their son, John. He would be my new big brother. He was "cool" and in high school.

So happily ever after, right? No! And very far from it. Starting that night and for the next seven years straight, John tortured and beat my sister, brother, and me. We would go to bed with empty stom-achs each night, waiting and wondering which of us he would pick first. We would know we were the chosen one when John slammed a baseball bat on one of our bodies while we huddled in our beds. That was our signal to follow John to his room, where he would hit, slap, and beat us until he got tired, and then he would force us to just stand still at the foot of his bed while he slept. The two that weren't chosen waited, knowing, they were next.

When I was about five years old, I remember John picked me first, two nights in a row. I was exhausted and bruised from the night before. Yet, I sat up as quickly as I could when I felt the slam of the bat on my shins. It was my stomach the night before. I tried not to cry, quickly rubbed my shins to feel for blood, and got up as fast as I could. John walked out, and I knew I better follow quickly. I saw my brother look at me with sympathy in his eyes; my sister pretended to keep sleeping. John pointed the bat at "the spot." I know this spot. The carpet was worn down from my little feet, with a bigger imprint from my sister and the biggest from my brother. The brown color camouflaged the blood left by us. I could feel the crunchiness of the carpet fibers from our tears, blood, and maybe even some urine. I did not know how long I would stand there this time. My whole body ached so badly. Yesterday, when he let me leave, the clock showed 2:27 AM.

Days turned into weeks and months into years as the abuse and neglect continued. The clothes on our backs were the same we had worn for years. The only food we ate was the free lunches provided by the school or what we could find from fruit trees or trashcans. The neighbor at the corner had a loquat tree and we would grab whatever we could from the branches that rested outside their fence. The family who lived three doors down usually threw away their boxes of cereal once a week. If we were lucky, they would leave the broken bits at the bottom of the bag. My sister would dole it out to the three of us. My favorite was the one that was shaped like a rectangle. I would not know what it tasted like to have the whole rectangle until ten years later.

TAKE ACTION AS IF YOU HAVE NOTHING TO LOSE

People often ask me how I managed to survive those years and keep going. How does anyone survive their chaotic childhoods? Trauma and pain do not discriminate and, unfortunately, are woven into everyone's life. Candidly, I was not physically strong nor was I especially brave. I, like many others, survived in the best way I could. I received daily messages that I was not deserving of love, not worthy of my basic needs to be met, and I didn't belong. Eventually, I believed those messages as truth. I didn't see another way of explaining my life up to then.

However, one pivotal event shifted my mindset and ultimately shaped my journey to this present day. One event that catapulted me into believing that taking action is sometimes all it takes. It all started when my biggest fear of being separated from my sister and brother came true. Even though John continued to torture us, in my young mind, I believed that being separated could be worse. Instead, we could each die horrible, excruciatingly painful deaths alone.

During school recess, my big sister told me she was running away and escaping to her friend's house. Her friend lived in a two-bedroom apartment with her six siblings and immigrant parents. They didn't have room for my brother or me. Instantly, my head, heart, and stomach felt jumbled. I didn't know what to do, so I walked home as usual. I knew John would be furious. What would he do to my brother and me? Would today be our last day alive?

As I walked home, a little girl from my class caught up with me. Maria had long, shiny brown hair and sparkly brown eyes. Her bubbly voice asked if I could stop at her house to play. I figured I had nothing more to lose anyway, so I followed Maria to her apartment and was instantly in awe. Her room had the coolest bunk bed, her kitchen filled with food, and a TV she casually flipped on to watch cartoons. I thought she was the luckiest girl in the world. She also made me a bologna sandwich on this fluffy white bread. I had never tasted anything so delicious.

Then I knew I had to go home. As predicted, John took out his anger on my brother and me that night because my sister was gone. The next day at school, when my sister saw my face swollen with bruises, she said, "You just have to ask anyone if you can live with them. Maybe they will say yes." The only person I could think of was Maria. I didn't know her well or how I would ask, but I knew I had to do it.

At lunchtime, I went up to her and blurted out, "Can I live with you?" Remember, we're in fifth grade. Looking back, I laugh at how awkward and ridiculous that must have sounded. Her response was the best. She said, "YES, but I think I have to ask my mom. She's at work. We can go to my house after school and call her." Her mom surprisingly said yes, and I remember the overwhelming relief I felt. I can't believe it. It worked!

This lady was a single mom raising two kids on her own in a very small apartment, willing to take on another child she just met. That first night at her house was the first of many things. The first time I received a hug and kiss good night, the first time I felt a soft pillow on my cheeks and a cozy blanket to cuddle in. It was the first time I heard, "I love you, sleep tight, see you in the morning." It was the first time someone offered me three meals in a day and asked me, "What do you want for dessert?"

BELIEVE IN THE *MAYBE*

Maria's mom fought to become my legal foster parent even though she did not qualify according to government standards. She showed me how believing in the maybe allowed me to stay with her as long as I did. She hoped that maybe the government would make an exception for us. She was not afraid of asking for help or taking action. Phone call after phone call, document after document would win us a month longer. Ultimately, they rejected her application because she was not married. Therefore, I would be moved to yet another foster home. We savored the rest of my stay with camping trips and summer parties. I even learned how to swim.

My time with Maria and her family taught me the power of believing in the "*maybe.*" Believing that something could be different opened up the possibility of something good happening. Of course, positive results are not guaranteed, but hope brings motivation to take the next step. Hope brought courage to ask for help, and maybe the worst won't happen. Believing in the maybe resulted in catching a glimpse of what my life could be like without feeling fearful of my life every night.

I realized I was stuck in that abusive foster home for so long because all I knew was how to endure. How many of us learned to endure because we couldn't see a way out? The thought of doing something to change my situation did not occur to me. I felt an unexplainable loyalty to my abusers. Do you know how baby elephants are trained? When they are young, they are tied to a tree. As they grow bigger and stronger, they stay tied to the tree even though they are strong enough to break free with a stomp. In some ways, I was a baby elephant tied to a tree in that abusive home.

After my escape, I would not let anything stop me from living a "normal" life. I was so accustomed to the look of disdain and disappointment. Once I learned how to get approval from others, I was addicted. According to psychiatrist,[1] who has written extensively on how trauma impacts the brain and the body, in survival mode, the human brain tends to operate in a highly mechanical manner, almost like a robot. Many adults like me who suffer from complex PTSD will try to cope by constantly striving, achieving, and wanting more to create a sense of worthiness[2]. At that time, I did not know I needed to heal my past; instead, I pushed the trauma aside as if it had never happened and met milestones, such as graduating from college, starting a career as a teacher, paying taxes, getting married, owning a dog, and starting a family. Everything looked good and right on track. I'm living the American dream, the life my immigrant parents probably dreamed about. My closet full of designer clothes said I was supposed to be happy, but I was not.

THE PAIN OF PRETENDING

My experience of constantly striving, achieving, and wanting more created a sense of superficial worthiness. However, the hard truth was I felt a deep disconnection within myself. I did not know what brings me happiness, so I followed the herd and did what others did. Soon after my daughter was born, post-partum depression hit hard. Even though my physical scars and bruises mostly healed, I found myself in complete distress. My therapist said I was experiencing complex PTSD from my childhood trauma, most likely triggered by the complicated birth of my daughter.

Additionally, I found myself grappling with what Silberg[3] terms the "anniversary effect"—a phenomenon that suggests when children reach the same developmental stage as when the parent experienced loss or abuse, it can trigger memories and unresolved grief for the parent. This made sense, as I felt completely overwhelmed by being a mom. I was so scared that I wasn't taking care of her properly. I stayed up most nights scared she would stop breathing.

Sleep deprivation, anxiety, and depression led me to believe there would be no end to the constant servicing of this little human. I went from being hyper-responsible in caring for my daughter to not caring at all. I assumed she would be taken away from me and live a horrible childhood just like me. I gave up. A more recent 2021 study in the Journal of the American Psychoanalytic Association continues to confirm that first-time mothers who experienced unstable or abusive childhoods often experienced increased anxiety and depression when their child reached the age at which the mother's own childhood trauma occurred.[4] I felt the burden of ending the cycle of generational trauma without the proper tools. How am I supposed to stop generational trauma when I started at a negative?

The only way I knew how to deal was either by pretending nothing was wrong or by distracting myself with whatever I could to numb the pain that was bubbling within me. Then, before I knew it, I was checking into an addiction rehabilitation facility. Soon after, my marriage ended in divorce. The façade of a "perfect life" was gone. I couldn't pretend anymore. My original solution of striving harder, achieving more, doing more, and buying more wasn't working anymore.

The pressure to be positive act happy, "be grateful," brought with it an overwhelming sense of guilt because I felt the exact opposite inside. I felt like a fraud. I was always waiting for the other shoe to drop, and it did. I was "being grateful" and "acting happy" for fear I would lose everything. In truth, I felt like the world hated me and I lashed out at everyone around me. This was the perfect recipe for a breakdown and broken relationships. My world as I knew it came to a full stop.

FROM FULL STOP TO UNSTOPPABLE

I spent some time feeling very sorry for myself and blaming others for my implosion. Eventually, I had to see that I was no longer a baby elephant tied to a tree yet again. With accountability came the realization that nobody will care more about me than me. Plain and simple. Nobody cares about all the mistakes I made in the past; they're too busy thinking about themselves and their mistakes. For the next decade, I dedicated myself to deep introspection and healing, which in turn opened space for true happiness and joy. This inspired me to go back to school to research how to help others do the same systematically.

If you were to scroll through my social media feed, one would think the whole world wants to wake up at 5 a.m., start a million-dollar side hustle while also vacationing on blue waters, and look perfect while doing so. My research showed the opposite. Most people surveyed have goals to simply work through their everyday issues and find joy in life with the least amount of discomfort and suffering.[5] Moreover, data shows in real life, most people struggle with typical life issues, such as recovering from an argument with a partner, embarrassing mistakes, or processing feelings of guilt and releasing shame. I was so excited because these are reachable goals for everyone!

When I received the opportunity to be a part of this book, I was overwhelmed by the feeling of being an imposter. The voice of my inner critic asked, "Why me?" My story is not the kind of story that goes "viral" on social media. I didn't start a huge company that made a gazillion dollars. But then I realized that is only a tiny percentage of our population that gets a disproportionate amount of attention. There is a quieter, yet larger percentage of people out there who are unstoppable simply by appreciating the act of living. For countless others and me, living an "ordinary," harmoniously peaceful life and maintaining it is an accomplishment that titans of their industry and global leaders of the world aspire to. While it may seem mundane to some, embracing the ordinary can be an extraordinary aspiration for many.

WHAT DOES UNSTOPPABLE MEAN TO YOU?

There are days when being "unstoppable" means waking up leisurely, getting up from my cozy bed, slowly brushing my teeth, sipping on a mug of hot chocolate, and gazing out my window for hours, enjoying my view. On other days, it's waking up with the first alarm, getting dressed in a power outfit, and hopping on a plane for a full day of productive meetings. An unstoppable life can be pressing on despite the daily twists and turns, savoring and celebrating the ups while extracting lessons from the downs that come with the roller coaster of life. It is not about forced gratitude or unwavering positivity and constantly striving to be number one. Sometimes, it is simply about showing up and being the best version of myself with the resources I have at that time. When challenges pop up, taking the next step, no matter how small, makes us all unstoppable.

A SYSTEMATIC APPROACH TO YOUR WELLNESS

If you have hit a roadblock in your life and are ready for a shift, this is the time to take an honest assessment of your past. Without consistently resetting and recalibrating our mindset, the little paper cuts to our hearts can turn into big gaping wounds. And a once-happy life can disintegrate. Although I designed The SISPEP Method to make the tiny shifts in our lives to prevent implosion, that doesn't mean implosions are "bad." It might be the catalyst we need to force us to assess if we are aligned with our truth to get to our next level.

The source of all our happiness and joy rests in our Spiritual, Intellectual, Social, Physical, Emotional, and Professional selves (SIS-PEP). Although I systematically mapped out a program, you do not need to be a participant to formulate your personal wellness program. In the world of an abundance of information, I highly recommend having a plan. Otherwise, you can spend years cherry-picking information and end up feeling as though you've gone in circles. Nothing wrong with going in circles or a few detours, but if you're feeling a time crunch like I was, here are five core principles I recommend in building your personalized program for yourself.

1. Baseline Assessment: What is your level of satisfaction with your wellness? What needs maintenance or improvement? What micro-actions are you willing to implement in your life to get results? Knowing your beginning allows you to map out your future even if it's just a week, month, or year out.

2. Go deep, real deep: What parts of you need healing that are difficult to face in your outside life? Just like whack-a-mole, when you heal one part, a different pain can pop up. Where have the past versions of you needed more attention and empathy? If you feel antsy during this time of introspection, do you feel worthy to dedicate time and space to focus solely on yourself? Self-reflection is your time to go deep without judgment.

3. Guidance: No one can argue that you are the expert in you. Eventually, you will find the answers. Asking for guidance could be considered as a way to fast-track your learnings about yourself and allow someone to see your blind spots. Do you lean towards evidence-based approaches and proven methodologies, or something tailored to meet unique needs and aspirations? Find people you trust to guide you.

4. Results: What is your return on investment of your time, energy, and finances that you expect to meet your goals? Do you simply want to feel better? How much better do you want to feel? Being clear about your expectations allows you to adjust your goals or your investment in yourself.

5. Strategize: What action steps will you need to take daily, weekly, monthly, or quarterly? How will you test? How long will you keep pushing through on the same plan before adjustments? When will it be okay to let go and cut your losses? The beauty of having a strategy is allowing it to be organic and shapeshift as you need. Gone are the days of simply sticking to a plan just because it was the original plan.

THERE IS NO END AND THAT'S OKAY

At the beginning of my healing journey, I naively believed that overcoming my past would lead to permanent peace and the end of all wanting. But I've come to realize there is no finite destination to healing or personal growth. Just because I was able to systematize a healing journey doesn't mean I don't experience triggers or go off the rails once in awhile. Acceptance of the humanness of our journey, reminds me to let go of the need to understand or control everything and instead return to the humble roots of believing in the magic of *"maybe."* Of maintaining hope, even when circumstances seem bleak. It means slowing down to listen deeply, speaking our truth clearly, and choosing decisions with intentionality. In the end, embracing the *"maybe"* and the *"what ifs"* allows us to be unstoppable in our acceptance of our authentic selves.

---

1. Van Der Kolk, B. A., & Van Der Kolk, B. (2015). *The body keeps the score: Brain, mind, and body in the healing of trauma.* Gildan Media Corporation.
2. Herman, J. L. (2019). *Trauma and recovery: The aftermath of violence--from domestic*
3. Silberg J. (2013). The Child Survivor: Helping Developmental Trauma and Dissociation. Routledge.
4. Sechi, C., Prino, L. E., Rollé, L., Lucarelli, L., & Vismara, L. (2021). Maternal attachment representations during pregnancy, perinatal maternal depression, and parenting stress: Relations to child's attachment. *International Journal of Environmental Research and Public Health, 19*(1), 69. doi:10.3390/ijerph19010069
5. Tam, L. (2020). *Exploring Mindfulness and Employee Engagement: An Innovation Study* (Doctoral dissertation, University of Southern California).

ABOUT DR. LILLY TAM

Dr. Lilly Tam is a regular speaker and enjoys conducting workshops with corporate teams.

Lilly is the founder of The SISPEP Method, which aims to help participants reset and recalibrate all six dimensions of their wellness. She lightheartedly considers herself a "mindset mechanic" because she enjoys working with clients to shift their mindset and make improvements in their lives, similar to fine-tuning a car. Lilly's research in employee engagement and mindfulness has shown positive results in work-life integration, conflict resolution, and confidence building. Her keynote and workshop, "Bombard Yourself With Your Truth," focuses on finding and healing the untruths reinforced by our inner critic. Lilly is a clinical hypnotherapist and received her Doctorate in Education from the University of Southern California.

Website: *www.LillyTam.com*
LinkedIn: *www.linkedin.com/in/lilly-tam*

9

LORIKAY COLEMAN

MAKE ANYTHING POSSIBLE!

I wish I had known thirty years ago what I know now... life would have been filled with more joy and ease as I transformed into using my personal power.

OVERVIEW

At my lowest times, my body wasn't functioning well. I felt worthless and incapable. I felt trapped, with no control, no ability to change things—trapped in my family, in my marriage, by my own self sabotage and by rigid beliefs. I felt misunderstood and so alone. My life felt heavy, as though I were wading through thick mud, dragging along with me so much baggage. Every step was a challenge.

I often felt an adversarial influence that did not want me to step into my full power. Through learning new techniques, I discovered that my subconscious programs from my childhood were weighing me down, and I seem to have inherited trauma patterns from my ancestors too!

Using clear intention and tapping into a fire within, I blazed a trail to release generational baggage and mindfully create new neural pathways and actions that support my body and spirit. This has helped me make anything possible.

I am deeply thankful for my tenacious spirit. I used to play a song called "Tubthumping:" "I get knocked down, but I get up again; you're never going to keep me down!" I would sing that at the top of my lungs, stepping into determination.

My story is one of triumph, as I learned to change how my mind views circumstances. I regularly deeply relax, giving evidence to my brain to rewire and strengthen new calming pathways for my nervous system and to help healing happen. I have embraced my gifts and personal power and have broken through major subconscious beliefs.

I have created a successful marriage, better health, as well as my Enlightened Life Path business that helps people lighten the burdens they are carrying, inspiring them to live to their highest potential. I help clear the path so transformational tools are effective and align the body and mind with the soul's desires, bringing more joy and peace to their lives.

FROZEN IN FEAR

My mother almost gave birth to me in the front seat of the car. She froze and didn't know what to do. I have come to realize that her fear was imprinted upon me, and freezing became my go-to response.

There have been times when my body was frozen after awakening from nightmares. I was conscious but not able to move. I'm thankful that I have been able to rewrite my birth experience through my hypnotherapy training, which has given me the ability to act more easily.

TRAPPED

As a baby with hip dysplasia, my foot was in a cast and my legs were placed in a brace that kept them spread open. This rigid structure created subconscious programs that taught me I had no power to change things and created an underlying theme of being trapped by an outside authority.

My father was an authoritarian. As a child, I felt like I was walking on eggshells with his explosive temperament and learned not to say much. When he came into a room, I would quickly jump up, ready to be told what to do. I felt I couldn't relax.

Growing up this way caused my senses to become hyper-aware, especially since I came to this earth with a sensitive body and spirit. Demeaning voice inflections would shatter me, and I would internalize harsh words which were directed to others. My father was very judgmental towards my mother, particularly concerning her weight. The texture of his voice registered in my body as disgust. Soon I had a recording of his voice replaying in my mind.

Later in life my sensitivity expressed as anxiety and contributed to the intensity of my allergies. (I have since learned to unravel the mixture of elements that create physical challenges, both for me and for others, which often helps the body function more optimally.)

QUEST FOR SAFETY

To me, the unknown was not safe. I recall trying to make my husband angry while we were dating so I could see what he was like. I was determined to find the most kind, calm man on the planet that was also humble and who maintained similar standards to mine.

Fortunately, I was successful in that quest, although I soon found myself overlaying my father's persona on my husband. I would tense up when it was time for him to come home and would relax when he left. I believed my thoughts were not important. My brain would freeze and shut down whenever I was asked questions. I often felt I needed to defend myself or simply felt stupid because I didn't have words to explain.

REWIRING MY NERVOUS SYSTEM

Luckily, I learned techniques for regaining my voice and changing my view of my husband. I call one of them "Redefining." I made two lists: first, a list of positive traits that I wanted to have my brain more easily recognize and be grateful for; and second, a list of things I did not want to focus on, including how my body felt around him.

Next, I did an aligning process that trained a part of my brain called the RAS to notice what I wanted. That process helped to rewire how my nervous system interacted with my husband, so that I experienced him differently and no longer felt trapped in my marriage, which now is more joyful and fulfilling.

LOSING THE USE OF MY HANDS

After my second son was born, I found it excruciatingly painful to grasp anything, as blisters and rashes would appear on my palms. As I served my children, I sent fiery anger at my hands which hurt so badly. Simply moving my hands or touching anything would also painfully trigger the most horrific itching response.

I later learned that we lived five miles downwind from an area that burned hazardous waste and that my symptoms were caused partly by heavy metals building up in me and food allergies; also by a compromised liver and a genetic condition that caused my body not to detoxify properly. I appreciated the cotton gloves given to me by my dermatologist, but his instruction not to touch anything and not be stressed was a joke!

However, I have learned much about de-stressing. I also learned that there are molecules of emotions with neuropeptides that can reconfigure themselves with a bit of intentional physical movement, which process emotions and reduce pain.

IGNORING INSPIRATION BRINGS PAIN

Just like my mother, I had no "off button" with sweets. I felt fat and wanted to lose weight. I ignored personal inspiration that I should not take the pills that were offered after a body-wrap.

Unfortunately, the diet pills ended up hurting my digestion. I had not yet realized that my body is extremely sensitive and can easily experience a myriad of negative effects from a number of causes.

After eating, fatigue washed over me, my brain became foggy, my body ached all over, rashes appeared and I had severe headaches, all while parenting two young boys from the bathroom throne!

Rage easily came. I pushed it deep inside. I didn't want to be like my father! I was determined not to have fiery energy that hurt others. However, one day I exploded and yelled at my three-year-old who dropped a gallon of milk that burst over the kitchen floor. On another occasion, something triggered me, and I grabbed a wooden spoon which left a bruise on his leg. I was devastated to realize that I had acted like my father. I determined then that I would become the chain breaker.

I learned to observe my behavior and say to myself, "This is what LoriKay feels like when she is angry." Then I would carefully notice things: tense neck, hot face, frantic darting eyes, wanting to run away. I needed to learn that it was safe for me to face what I feel.

Much later I learned to create power from my anger when I saw injustices, and in a calm and focused way was able to bless the lives of many who were homeless. During this period, I was prompted to invite two people, at different times, to come and live with me for a while in order to help them turn their lives around.

WANTING TO END IT ALL

As a young mother, I really hoped that God would remove my trials. Now I understand the growth and gifts I developed as he led me at a pace that I was willing to take.

As the years went by, there were times when I was able to flow towards faith and hope and could feel my burdens lifted. However, other times my mindset would spiral down drastically.

Adversarial influences seemed to magnify any negative thought a hundred-fold. There was one very dark day when it seemed that the pain and frustration of caring for a one- and a three-year-old was more than I could do.

I wanted everything to end and immediately had an idea of how to do it in a painless way. The heaviness and darkness surrounded me, and I was on a slippery slope of suicidal thoughts. Miraculously a church member called, and the ringing telephone snapped me out of that dangerous thought pattern.

CHOOSING HOW TO LIVE

Soon I recognized that this life is about learning to choose where to focus. I tried focusing on giving my burdens to Christ, on having gratitude, and serving others. Sometimes I was just too tired to do anything and chose to look up and focus on my ceiling, feeling grateful that it was clean!

I believe that part of the reason we come to this earth is to learn what it's like to experience opposites. I want to use my agency to choose the better part, but sometimes we aren't as free as we think, as we carry so much baggage.

Some of our baggage is from subconscious programs. I carried a belief from my ancestors' experiences of being powerless to change things. I chose to experience freedom and power to change things in the silliest ways to prove to my brain that I can: I smiled and laughed while turning on a light switch. Doing actions with emotion helps to rewire the brain, and I enjoy celebrating that I can easily change things.

I also celebrate being free to move. Having worked through my body image issues, I now have videos of myself leading classes. I hope you can join me some time to learn simple movements that help the subtle energy flow while doing some brain rewiring techniques and guided visualization.

I believe that my spirit agreed to have my body so I could learn specific lessons and experience the growth that my soul desired and could learn to clear the ancestral powerless pattern. When we break free of a habit or belief that was initiated by an ancestor, it helps them opt into being more free, and sometimes they then can be more helpful to us on earth!

I also had a strong belief that life was hard. I had heard this expressed at church. My father was born during the depression, and during most of my life I felt poor. I believed money should be saved. I felt so much guilt paying for medical help when I became sick.

Sometimes our baggage doesn't allow us to accept help. A friend suggested a doctor three hours away, but I couldn't imagine getting past the obstacles of the drive, babysitters and the money. She also suggested I stop eating wheat, milk, corn, soy and sugar. I didn't want to make those kinds of changes! Ironically, after suffering for a couple more years, I learned to eat that way and to value my ability to function over what my taste buds wanted.

Even with my best efforts, I had chronic fatigue, often was in pain, and continued to struggle with the skin on my hands. I realized that my identity (and my self-worth) was directly related to how much I served others. Eventually I learned the lesson God was trying to teach me: "I have value because I *exist*, not because I *do*."

UNFINISHED CONVERSATIONS

I've certainly been on a journey. I now am stronger, more resilient, and have greater access to my personal power. I remember trying different kinds of yoga, and one that incorporated *mudras* and *mantras* especially resonated with me. It involves different finger positions that allow the energy to flow through helpful circuits while chanting sounds—which calm the vagus nerve and open the throat *chakra,* making it easier to say what is needed. I enjoy leading these kinds of classes.

Yoga was changing me for the better, but it was an adjustment for my family. My father wasn't used to the new LoriKay who would not bend over backwards in response to his every demand. I had always enjoyed serving, but I now was a very busy mother of four. I recall one time when he was livid that I could not help him immediately.

After he stormed out, I asked God to help bring my father's higher self for me to talk to. As I imagined that happening, I spoke to him, repeating over and over: "I hear you. You hear me. I understand you. You understand me." My imaginary conversation with my father resulted in each of us feeling loved. I transformed anger into healing as I radiated compassion and forgiveness. Within an hour, he called me and apologized—for the first time ever!

Are there people in your life with whom you have unfinished conversations? I recall making a huge list of people from my past where I didn't get to say what I needed to. Doing this simple process will bring momentum to your progress!

Imagine rowing a boat with twenty-five anchors tossed over the side of the boat. Each unfinished conversation slows you down as you try to move forward!

FIRING GOD

My relationship with God has at times been a rocky one. It's funny how I have viewed Christ as a helpful support and God the Father as a demanding God who doesn't show love in helpful ways. I recognize that I had overlaid my own father's traits onto God, perceiving God as demanding and punishing.

After my father passed away, it seemed as though a Pandora's box opened, and I experienced severe anxiety. One day I was driving a church member to a doctor's appointment. He smelled like smoke, and I felt trapped in a poisoned container.

My right leg was cramping severely. I used my tools to communicate with my body—gently rubbing the area, asking what it needed, saying in my mind, "I'm sorry, please forgive me, I love you." I imagined breathing Christ's light and love into it, and the pain as a color and a shape leaving my body. When he left the car, I started sobbing and shaking, realizing how traumatizing it was to feel like I was trapped serving him. That experience was enough, finally, to get me to be willing to pay for professional help.

My therapist felt I had not yet processed small traumas, let alone big ones. I kept disassociating as I did EMIR (a process that helps release traumatic memories). There was a week when every night I felt I was being choked as the muscles in my throat started reliving memories. During this time I recalled my parents sharing that I had once had my stomach pumped. That helped me to put context to the experience.

In this difficult phase of life, I would wake up, call out to God in my mind and ask for light to open my throat. I was angry when help didn't come quickly. It was so frightening! I used Emotional Freedom Technique to process my thoughts, and to help my meridian channels open and allow *chi* to flow through my body more easily, ten minutes of this felt like an eternity!

Honestly, during this time, I became *incredibly* ticked at Heavenly Father. I wanted a God who felt supportive. One time I prayed, "Hey you, you suck; the end!" I felt abandoned and believed He didn't care. I no longer wanted that kind of God.

REDEFINING GOD

Eventually I took every belief I had about God and religion, examined it, redefined things, did the Cellular Alignment Technique, and now carry loving, supportive beliefs.

I believe there are divine beings who created this universe as an advanced school for us to learn to choose the higher path of love and are here to partner with us to transform our experiences into valuable wisdom. I am held by a greater power than myself all the time. Christ is there to lighten my burdens, and I am surrounded by an angelic team who love and protect me.

I'm so happy that I have been able to sense the spirit of my father and have even trained my nervous system to experience him in more positive ways. He was supportive, provided for his family, instilled a great work ethic in me, wanted me to enjoy life, and loved me in the best way he could, even as he was living in tremendous physical pain. I have great compassion and gratitude for him!

REWIRING

Since 2010, I have helped others with anxiety, depression and pain and have helped their bodies to function more optimally. Now I also help people to become **unstoppable** in reaching their goals and learning to understand their personal strengths and purpose. The Cellular Alignment Technique I teach has helped hundreds to move through self-sabotage.

Sometimes we tend to act as though we're addicted to part of our programming; that is, what is *known* and therefore safe. The opposite of this is metaphorically running away from what may be helpful. Since it is *not known*, it therefore is not safe. The technique helps make new neural pathways that give evidence of safety. This works with all kinds of goals: financial, physical and relationship.

I've combined my knowledge into a powerful formula which helps a person to move forward, having more freedom and joy as they put themselves in a place of CHOICE. The technique takes care of the "STOPPERS"—those things that tend to divide the efforts you put in towards achieving a goal.

I have some free training to share with you. It's much easier to show than to write out! For now, however, I will share the formula along with a brief description:

$$Make\ Anything\ Possible = Spirit\ Connection + Intent\ \frac{(Learn + Apply + Focus)}{(STOPPERS)}$$

<u>SPIRIT CONNECTION</u>:
First connect to
(1) your higher self
(2) your Higher Power
(3) your angelic team

Next imagine loving light coming down from heaven and filling you. Connecting to a Higher Power or the Universe and taking actions to remove blocks are key to being unstoppable. (I easily work with all belief systems.)

<u>INTENT</u>: What do you want?
To be unstoppable, often we need to <u>LEARN</u> a skill.
Obviously, we also need to <u>APPLY</u> what we learn.

<u>FOCUS</u>: There are two kinds of FOCUS. A softer focus is more meditative and includes imagining things being what you want. The other is a determined focus that is directed to specific tasks. The technique makes it possible to be better at applying the right kind of focus when needed.

<u>STOPPERS</u>: Our baggage that can be magnified by adversarial influence, which does not want us to grow to our full potential:

Subconscious programs running and Conscious mind not present.
Trauma: life experiences from earlier ages that weren't processed.
Other people's mental and emotional energy and their actions.

Parents and ancestors: experiences of our ancestors that have been passed down.

Physical body: Issues with body's systems, nerve connection, blood flow.

Energy body issues in chakras/meridians/aura.

Rehashing events and thoughts.

Soul wound: experiences that happened before this life.

ALIGNING TECHNIQUE

We use our conscious mind to hold a specific intent while doing different breathing patterns and tapping sequences. I call it "Aligning." This brings blood flow to the prefrontal cortex (away from the primitive brain), while giving input to the reticular activating system (the filter in the brain that decides what is important to bring to our awareness). This part of the brain starts finding solutions. The breath pattern also makes it easier to be motivated to move forward towards goals and is energizing. In time it will also begin to strengthen new neural pathways.

This process helps you step into a place to act and not be acted upon, as it lessens the Stoppers' ability to hinder efforts, making progress easier and not relying on sheer willpower to achieve what is wanted.

It has been fun changing what appears impossible into what is actually achievable with this technique. For example, I hosted a World Empowering Transformation Summit with Zoom. It was a huge task, especially considering that I had zero technology skills, and my brain would shut down in front of a computer! I successfully moved through the barriers and ultimately received feedback that the teachings had positively helped women around the world.

With this alignment technique I have helped clients bring in money, make progress with a new business, improve relationships, let past lovers go, be empowered to be around others, accept differences in family members' beliefs and gender roles, stop smoking and overcome porn addictions.

Making progress can be easier!

It's kind of human nature to forget how far we have progressed. Taking note of where we started is helpful, then learning to focus on the gains we've made and celebrating that progress, rather than focusing on the gap, noticing only how far the ideal situation appears to be from where we are. I'm truly in awe at my progress.

STAR METHOD

As I was sick with COVID, the STAR method came into my mind clearly. It has proven very transformative. I'm offering a Success Membership where you can join me monthly to experience the Alignment technique and STAR method.

S= Stimulate the physical body in a way that helps the energy body flow.
T=Tap into your higher power and higher self
A=Aligning Technique
R=Rewire and Rewrite the story

BLESSINGS

I'm thankful for all the things I have learned and for the inspiration I received concerning what to do. One time when I was frustrated about the speed of my hands' recovery, I felt I should write as if my hands could talk to me. During this practice, I softened my eye focus, allowed my eyelids to droop down, and then imagined that my hands had a voice. I then wrote, "All you do is send anger to me. Don't you know I'm trying to serve you the best I can?" I now emphasize the importance of self-compassion as well as gratitude.

I believe that with God's help I have moved forward, despite the package my body came in and despite the environment in which I was placed. I received a priesthood blessing in which I was told that I was to work hard on a special talent with which I had been gifted and that my hands would be dexterous in helping others.

I have been blessed to hold onto my Christian faith *while* expanding and learning about:

- Using Human Design and Soul Astrology to help myself and others become aware of when actions are out of alignment, understand strengths, and life purpose.
- How to send healing energy to anyone anywhere.
- Deep focus and directing molecules to change so the body functions more optimally.
- Energy work to let go of generational patterns.
- Removing adversarial influences with spiritual help.
- Clearing negative or heavy energy from food and in homes.
- Using the symbolism of colorful balls flowing away to help release negative energy.
- Removing subconscious baggage with hypnotherapy.
- The power of breath to invite life force energy through the chakras and meridian channels.
- Humming or chanting "Om" for relaxation.
- Gentle body movements to release stress and reduce pain.
- Brain rewiring techniques.

SUMMARY

I have learned so many wonderful things that give me peace regardless of what is happening in the outside world. My new mantra is, "I relax and trust that I'm in the flow of doing what needs to be done to evolve the world and have the energy to sustain my actions."

I'm excited to share ways to break through subconscious programs, resolve some of the stuck nonbeneficial generational patterns and optimize subtle energy flow so that growth can more easily happen.

There are many ways to help clear interference. I have videos showing how gentle movement mingled with visualization can help to release what is stuck in the physical or energetic body. I also have group hypnotherapy sessions that help actions be more effective. I hope you will join me in the Success Membership and receive these bonuses.

Many like to work with the masses. I still enjoy the one-on-one approach. I enjoy shining light on the divine potential of others, shedding light on their purpose. I love helping others achieve what they desire while experiencing more peace, joy, and compassion for themselves.

I have better health, growth with my business, and more fulfilling relationships as I've taken steps to make anything possible. I'd love to help you do the same! Connect with me to receive free training where I show the basic part of the alignment technique.

I'd also be happy to create a personalized program specific to your needs. It would be my privilege to work with you closely to obtain your desired goals and become **unstoppable**!

Access Free Alignment Technique Training here:

ABOUT LORIKAY COLEMAN

LoriKay is a heart-centered success coach who helps clients embrace their divine potential and achieve their desires. She helps turn on a "success switch" in the brain, works with the subconscious, the physical and subtle energy body and releases negative generational patterns. Her approach is an alchemy of mind, body and spirit work that brings love, joy and peace and teaches transformational techniques that rewire the brain to stop self-sabotage and improve physically, mentally or achieve goals more easily. With her Enlightened Life Path business, she brings light to clients' paths and joyful lightness into their lives. She's certified in Hypnotherapy, NLP, QiGong and FootZoning. She is also a Reiki Master, Abundance Masters Coach, Cellular Alignment Teacher and Energy Healing/Four Pathways Professional. LoriKay teaches the "Make Anything Possible Formula" that brings the body, mind and spirit into alignment with what is wanted. She lives in Arizona with her husband (celebrating 35 years), has four children, with her youngest currently serving a church mission.

Website: *www.enlightenedlifepath.com*
FREE Alignment Technique Training: *www.enlight enedlifepath.com/FREE-Technique-Training*
Discounted Success Membership: *www.enlight enedlifepath.com/success-membership*
YouTube: *www.youtube.com/@enlightenedlight path3901*

MARIA MILITSOPOULOU

EMPOWERING WOMEN: REDEFINING ROLE MODELS

I remember from a young age being asked, **"Who are your role models?** Which women do you admire? Whom do you aspire to be like?"

My answer was always the same: "I don't have role models!"

All the figures that elicited admiration, curiosity, and served as a source of inspiration for me were men.

In art, in politics, in writing, in innovation, and in science... ALL MEN. I come from a generation where all role models were shaped according to an Alpha Dominant Male form that left little room for deviation.

It took many evolutionary years and an incredibly revealing journey filled with twists and turns, human stories rich in connectivity patterns, metaphors, and spirituality for me to understand that role models do not have to do with how famous you have become. Instead, it's how powerful the struggle you give every day in the game of survival is, enough to be a source of inspiration and a driving force for other people regardless of gender!

Today, the answer to the same question after four incredible decades full of action, cinematic twists, and endless human communication has changed... Role models, but also a source of inspiration for me, are ALL those women who in the 21st century STILL FIGHT EVERY DAY for their rights, who try to keep the institution of the family alive alongside their professional pursuits in a truly hostile professional arena, in a modern life that DEMANDS you to give 100% of your time divided into endless obligations in an endless effort not to lose your identity and with an even greater stake not to LOSE your soul somewhere along the way!

To all these women, I dedicate today my own chapter as a contribution to the UNSTOPPABLE rise of female leaders, and at the same time, I dedicate it to a very unique person, who took a lot of work for me to be able to love her as she deserves, Maria... because the most difficult part towards transcendence is to learn how to respect and love yourself.

SEEDS OF EMPOWERMENT: STORIES BEYOND SELF-PROMOTION AND TRIUMPHS

The invitation was wonderful – an opportunity to contribute to an inspiring book where women from different parts of the world who have conquered their personal peaks and have even made their dreams a reality, will share knowledge, experiences, and real stories of female empowerment.

The true objective here isn't simply about self-promotion or reveling in accomplishments; it lies in the genuine stories that shape each personal journey and guide individuals toward essential lessons. Through these straightforward narratives, a "SEED" must travel in order to discover its place either within the mind or the heart of the receiver.

At this point, it always depends on how the brain patterns of each recipient function, as the heart needs emotional stimuli and the brain facts to support the storytelling with real life examples. However, the essence remains the same—a seed of knowledge will give the inspiration and strength that the soul needs to continue its journey and reach its highest destination.

BRIDGING THE GAP BETWEEN PERCEPTION AND REALITY

I always remember, from my teenage years, hearing about the glamorous stories of successful women with a reservation, blaming it on my neuro-structures. I've always craved facts to believe in anything. I recall seeing magazine covers and photos from events with beautiful, radiant women, exuding a dynamic gaze, well-dressed and framed by stunning cinematic settings; and around them, people seemed to support their success. It all seemed perfect, like a dream!

I always thought about how I would conquer a dream! Yes, I'm the visual type; images and neuromarketing worked in harmony, creating the right conditions for me to have reasons to strive and one day capture my own ideal photos!

Fast forward to today, after an incredibly metaphysical orchestrated journey filled with ups and downs and daily adventures, my dreams have become a reality, and I too, have acquired a corresponding archive of beautiful photos and covers, depicting my journey to success.

However, what we truly need to share with all women around us is not just the beautiful moments or the final outcome, but the dark, even very dark and truly difficult points along the path of a road that was NEVER and FOR NO ONE paved with rose petals, open doors to success, and people ready to lend a helping hand! The naked truth is far from this, and we need to share the whole story in the name of Women Empowerment, offering women a complete view of a professional journey, rather than just glamorous moments of the final destination.

NAVIGATING CHALLENGES IN MOTHERHOOD AND LEADERSHIP

The previous evening, I pondered which inspired story of female leadership I should share with the public. Among the many wonderful stories of real challenges, it was truly difficult to pick one particularly unique. The answer came to me on its own, as it always does, to pull me out of the same deadlock, that very same night at 4:00 am. As I contemplated, I found myself covered in vomit, cradling a sweet, exhausted baby in my arms, suffering from high fever, seeking comfort and relief. Meanwhile, the laptop remained open, awaiting the continuation of reports I should have already submitted the previous week, documents I needed to read by the next afternoon, and my body exhausted from insomnia, physical fatigue, and hormonal imbalances accompanying a woman's body after an extended period of breastfeeding.

What really goes on in a woman's mind during such moments? The truth?

Under other circumstances, pressure, sadness, inadequacy, collapse—everything you want to do but can't find the time for and for all the things you take on, willingly or unwillingly, but time is never enough. With the baby in my arms, the laptop still open, and my body under exhaustion, the voice inside me came strong and sure, guiding me once more on the path of Resilience that we both me and "Maria" consciously chose, implementing the mechanisms of transcendent protocols and executing what MUST be done.

In this mode, the mechanism demands swift decisions, setting a mental list of tasks and delegating if possible to supportive teams, like a partner, family, or supporting staff if available. But if there's no one but You, and I address the women who raise their children alone, my true heroines, then again there's a way rooted in mindfulness and resilience.

In the structures of resilience, the strategy is mandatory. If you don't have it as a natural inclination, then you MUST learn how to do it, because in life from going to the supermarket to standing in the boardroom it takes strategy, a skill that all women should learn from a young age, adapting it to their personality.

Most of the time, everything feels like an Unbearable burden, but we must never forget that as a species, we're designed to "survive."

At the end of this chapter, I know which question will be the most popular: "How easy is it to practice mindfulness while covered in vomit?" Yes, it can be possible and part of a success plan.

Though images like the ones I described above are familiar to women all over the planet they're certainly never described in the context of leadership, yet they're directly related to the battles women fight daily worldwide, in an attempt to achieve the impossible within a structured social framework that demands more and more, giving in return little crumbs as a driving force that discreetly activates a mental hamster wheel that doesn't truly lead anywhere!

As for the question of what kind of leadership I've chosen to apply to my personal journey of female leadership, the answer, after many trials and tribulations, has been clear and fully conscious for years: Transcendence Leadership.

JOURNEY THROUGH THE SENSES: A TEST OF FAITH

I must admit that since a young age, I always felt comfortable in leadership roles, and it happened in a natural way. As it was later revealed through the journey of self-discovery, it was like a trait encoded in my neural pathways. However, as I always say, when teaching Leadership to the developing leaders of tomorrow, it's not enough just to have a gift; from the moment you identify it, you must cultivate it until you learn how to leverage it to its fullest potential! Success always comes in a challenging way, but what's important is to recognize that failures and difficult trials that occur during the "journey" are part of the training!

My training towards transcendent leadership unfolded in a beautifully enlightening metaphysical way...!

It all started in the middle of 2015. A simple flu became the trigger to permanently losing two of my five senses—smell and taste just vanished!

At first, I thought everything would return to normal and that it was just temporary. However, months later, with endless medical examinations, both domestically and internationally, and countless visits to doctors of various specialties, the answer from all sources was the same: "You must learn to live with this."

Your senses have been destroyed! It's rare that this happens at such a young age, but there's nothing that can be done. The situation is irreversible!

This "irreversible" hit my ears like a curse for someone who created memories through scents and flavors. Not feeling anything at all was simply tragic. I couldn't understand anything, and even if the room next to me was set on fire I wouldn't notice.

Everything seemed to have died out... gone, like all the beautiful scents of nature, I couldn't smell my baby anymore, my favorite scents, like the taste of coffee that I loved; everything I ate simply left a muddy sensation in my mouth; and my naturally positive and happy mindset, was challenged as I found myself facing an incredible struggle that could shake my faith. And as my doctors informed my family, they should watch for signs of depression that might arise!

From the beginning, I didn't understand that this was all part of a "Training," and even though I was a spiritual person from a young age, I became embittered, stubborn, my heart hardened, filled with anger and rage. Not being able to have something forever was something I couldn't accept with my human ego. I started processes of prayer every day with a program.

I decided that by strengthening my spiritual structures, I would bring everything back.

After all, it wouldn't be the first time that a "miracle" came into my life... My entire existence was a series of miracles; I was familiar with it through many different wonderful metaphysical ways. So, I felt so sure that this would also happen now, whenever the factor of FAITH was missing. Therefore, dedication of time and commitment to the goal were crucial, and I felt so sure that this was simply enough. How wrong was I!

EMBRACING THE PATH TO TRANSCENDENT LEADERSHIP: LESSONS LEARNED THROUGH SPIRITUAL AWAKENING

As time went by, my faith remained unwavering. Each day, I faithfully observed my spiritual procedures. There were moments of doubt, when I felt mentally drained from striving endlessly for what seemed unattainable. This struggle had consequences on both my professional and personal life, particularly during this trying period when my prayers appeared to go unanswered for the first time.

Instead of surrendering to despair, I sought to understand where I went Wrong.

It was clear that my efforts weren't working well, so I doubled down on my dedication, even adding fasting to my spiritual routine. This change was quite different, especially for someone like me who usually depended on logic. The more I tried to improve myself, the more problems I faced.

During this special journey, I kept learning from difficult situations. While talking about my precarious situation with friends, coworkers, and random people, I became someone they trusted with their serious health problems, even worse than mine. Every day, I heard a lot about struggling.

Rather than withdrawing or allowing negativity to consume me, I chose to intercede on behalf of these individuals through prayer. As the list of those in need expanded, a remarkable occurrence unfolded: individuals joined me united around this cause, forming groups committed to communal prayer for the recovery of strangers.

Yes, forming purpose-driven groups had always been a cornerstone of my leadership journey, starting from my university days.

These groups united individuals, each contributing their positive energy and sharing requests for assistance from people across the globe. The outcomes were nothing short of remarkable. Every participant in the prayer chains during that period witnessed miracles unfold in their lives. From individuals in dire circumstances, like a child in a coma or a stranger recovering in the hospital after an accident, to countless others, healing became a reality. Each success story brought immense positivity and fulfillment to all those who were involved.

Spiritually, I felt uplifted every day, as if reaching towards the heavens. My soul was filled with an extraordinary sense of peace and joy, safeguarding me from the impact of any negativity around me. However, there was one notable exception – I never sought healing for myself. Instead, my focus remained on coordinating the groups, offering encouragement, sharing experiences to support others, and spreading the uplifting news of healings to others. Even as I continued to dedicate myself to this higher purpose, I couldn't help but wonder about my own situation.

It had been two and a half years of this spiritual journey when, during a fervent prayer session, I finally acknowledged my own need for healing, surrendering to a higher power, accepting whatever outcome awaited me. Later that same day, during a family dinner, suddenly, my senses returned to normal, even more intensely than before... The flavors and aromas of the meal were more vivid than ever, and I was filled with an overwhelming sense of happiness and gratitude.

Through this profound experience, I learned to begin my everyday with gratitude, appreciating even the simplest of joys. Embracing this lesson was challenging, particularly as I remained steadfast in my leadership role, ensuring the well-being and unity of those under my care. Yet, even more challenging was prioritizing others' well-being over my own, without expecting anything in return.

Six months later, I have made another dream into a reality—the creation of my own company. But this journey wasn't defined by a single experience; rather, it was shaped by a lifetime of spiritual and metaphysical encounters, guiding me from my earliest days to the present. This particular challenging experience led me to embrace transcendent leadership and recognize the importance of sowing the SEEDS of goodness, uniting people under a noble cause.

REFLECTIONS ON TRANSCENDENT LEADERSHIP

As I settle into my chair to pen down my thoughts on transcendent leadership, I find myself reflecting on the myriad experiences and insights that have shaped my belief in its transformative power. This isn't just a discourse on leadership theory; it's a narrative of my personal journey—a journey that has brought me to a profound understanding: transcendent leadership isn't merely the zenith of leadership; it's the catalyst that molds the leaders of tomorrow.

To me, transcendent leadership symbolizes the peak of leadership evolution. It transcends the conventional of authority and directive, guiding leaders towards a deeper sense of purpose and interconnectedness with the world around them.

At its essence, transcendent leadership embodies spirituality, vision, service, ethics, integrity, authenticity and personal growth, composing them into a mosaic of excellence.

In a world marked by swift change, uncertainty, and interdependence, the need for transcendent leadership has never been more pressing. Traditional leadership paradigms, fixated on immediate gains and hierarchical structures, falter in confronting the multifaceted challenges of our era.

Transcendent leadership, however, offers a holistic, future-directed approach—a beacon of light in the modern world.

One of its distinguishing features is its emphasis on visionary foresight and forward-thinking. Transcendent leaders aren't content with merely managing the present; they harbor a vivid vision of a brighter future and inspire others to share that vision. They anticipate challenges and opportunities, navigating a path towards tomorrow's promise.

Another trademark of transcendent leadership is its commitment to service and empowerment. Transcendent leaders prioritize the welfare of others, fostering ecosystems of trust, collaboration, and shared purpose. They empower individuals to harness their unique talents, fostering a sense of ownership and collective achievement.

At the core of transcendent leadership lies ethical integrity—a steadfast adherence to principles of fairness, justice, and sustainability. Even in the face of adversity, transcendent leaders uphold their values, setting a moral compass for others to follow.

Yet, perhaps the most profound aspect is its focus on personal growth and transformation. Transcendent leaders understand that authentic leadership begins within; they embark on a journey of self-discovery and mastery, cultivating virtues of resilience, authenticity, and humility.

Looking ahead, in a world ripe with uncertainty and change, the leaders of tomorrow will be tasked with navigating uncharted waters with wisdom and compassion. Transcendent leadership equips them with the mindset and tools needed to rise to this challenge, tapping into their full potential to inspire greatness and forge a brighter tomorrow for generations to come, bring about positive change and create a brighter future for us all.

BEYOND BOUNDARIES: INSPIRING TALES OF TRANSCENDENT LEADERSHIP

Amidst the vast landscape of transcendent leadership, let me narrate an example that resonates deeply—a story of a woman whose leadership transcended boundaries and inspired transformation on a monumental scale.

Think about the story of Sarah, a remarkable woman who exemplifies transcendent leadership in action. Sarah's journey began in a male-dominated industry, where she encountered countless obstacles and challenges. Despite the daunting odds stacked against her, Sarah refused to conform to the status quo. Instead, she embraced her unique perspective and saw it as an opportunity to catalyze innovation and drive positive change within her organization.

Sarah's leadership style was characterized by empathy, inclusivity, and a profound commitment to serving others. Recognizing the importance of diversity and representation, she actively sought out opportunities to mentor and empower women in her industry. Through her guidance and support, Sarah inspired a new generation of female leaders to rise to prominence, breaking through the glass ceiling that had long hindered their progress.

Despite facing resistance and skepticism from some quarters, Sarah remained unwavering in her convictions. Guided by her deeply held ethical principles and vision for a more equitable future, she persisted in her efforts to effect meaningful change. Her resilience and determination served as a beacon of hope for those around her, inspiring them to join her in the pursuit of a shared vision.

As time passed, Sarah's efforts began to bear fruit. Tangible shifts in her organization's culture and practices became evident, with more women ascending to leadership positions and diversity and inclusion becoming central tenets of the company's ethos. Through her tireless advocacy and dedication, Sarah had succeeded in effecting a profound transformation within her organization, leaving an indelible mark on its trajectory for years to come.

Transcendent leadership isn't merely a theoretical construct; it's a lived experience—an ongoing journey of growth, discovery, and service. It's about recognizing the interconnectedness of all beings and the responsibility we have to each other and the planet we inhabit.

As we delve deeper into the essence of transcendent leadership, it's essential to explore its various dimensions and how they manifest in real-world scenarios. Visionary foresight, for instance, is a hallmark of transcendent leadership. Leaders who possess this quality aren't content with the status quo; they envision a future that transcends current limitations and inspires others to join them on the journey towards realizing that vision.

Take, for instance, Malala Yousafzai, the Pakistani activist for female education and the youngest Nobel Prize laureate. Malala's unwavering commitment to girls' education in the face of adversity exemplifies transcendent leadership. Despite facing threats to her life from the Taliban, Malala remained resolute in her mission, advocating for the rights of girls to receive an education.

Malala's vision extended beyond her own personal safety; she saw education as a catalyst for societal transformation, empowering girls to break free from the cycle of poverty and oppression. Through her courageous activism, Malala inspired millions around the world to stand up for justice and equality, proving that age is no barrier to making a difference.

Another dimension of transcendent leadership is ethical integrity—a commitment to upholding moral principles even in the face of adversity. Leaders who possess this quality are guided by a deep sense of right and wrong, and they strive to make decisions that align with their values, even when it's challenging to do so.

Yet another dimension of transcendent leadership is personal growth and transformation. Leaders who embrace this aspect of leadership recognize that true change begins within. They commit themselves to a journey of self-discovery and continuous improvement, striving to become the best versions of themselves so that they can inspire others to do the same.

Transcendent leadership isn't just a lofty ideal; it's a practical approach to leadership that has the power to transform individuals, organizations, and societies. By embracing principles such as visionary foresight, ethical integrity, and personal growth, leaders can inspire positive change and create a brighter future for all. As we navigate the complexities of the modern world, let us strive to embody the spirit of transcendent leadership and lead with compassion, courage, and conviction.

A TOAST TO POSITIVE GLOBAL CHANGE

As I bring this personal chapter on female leadership to its close, I extend a heartfelt toast. With the crystal champagne glass raised high, let us salute the incredible women who grace our world. To those who surpass themselves daily, conquering their personal picks and navigating the delicate balance of time and inner harmony.

A salute to their tireless efforts to leave a legacy while giving birth and nurturing the future generations to embody the essence of resilience and determination.

And what does this toast's crystal glass contain?

It's not champagne that fills this glass but something equally refreshing and invigorating and so precious, cold, refreshing, mineral water that we must savor sip by sip in a mindful way as a reminder that the most beautiful and precious things in life are often disregarded every day because we take them for granted until we lose them.

Today, give yourself a couple of minutes to enjoy a glass of cold water as if you were tasting it for the first time. Take notice of the way the light reflects off the surface of the water.

Bring the glass to your lips and take a small sip. Close your eyes. Notice the sensation of the water entering your mouth, feel the texture, the aroma, the taste, and the sense of pleasure it offers you with its simplicity.

Slowly swallow the water and pay attention to the feeling as it travels down your throat into your stomach.

Take another sip, this time focusing on the sensations even more intensely. Notice any thoughts or feelings that arise as you drink the water.

Once you've finished drinking, take a moment to appreciate the experience. Notice how you feel physically and mentally. Finally express gratitude for the simple pleasure of drinking water and for taking the time to practice it in a mindful way.

And this, ladies, is part of transcendence.

Wishing you all blessings and soon to discover your true mission, spending the time on this training planet that we call Earth in the most meaningful way.

With appreciation,
Maria M.

ABOUT MARIA MILITSOPOULOU

Maria Militsopoulou is a multi-awarded Inspirational Female Transcendent Leader and Founder of Women Empowerment World-wide Leadership (WEWiL.global). She is also the Founder and CEO/CVO of YouDream TECH HUB, a future-oriented Tech Company with a vast international network of specialized professionals providing cutting-edge innovative solutions partnering with Tech Organizations at the forefront of the Global Tech Industry.

As a Motivational Speaker and an Author, she is committed to fostering women's empowerment, teaching and mentoring Positive Transcendent Leadership to women worldwide. She has also created the Tech Hub, the Dreamjob Platform, as well as the HR Hybrid Model Innovation.

Websites: www.mmilitsopoulou.com
www.womenempowermentworldwideleadership.com
LinkedIn: www.linkedin.com/in/maria-militsopoulou-
innovation-management-digitalmarketing-technol
ogy-venturecapital-startups

11

DR. NANCY MOREHOUSE

EMBRACING NEURODIVERGENCE, STRATEGIC RISK, AND LIVING FEARLESSLY

Life's challenges are not supposed to paralyze you; they are supposed to help you discover who you are.

— BERNICE JOHNSON REAGON

THE QUESTION I COULD NOT ANSWER

"**I want you to name five things in the room that begin with the letter S,**" **the neurologist asked.** After a long pause to process this instruction, which I later was told was over two minutes, the doctor said, "Just try to come up with any words that began with an S." I remember trying to make my mouth say the words I could so clearly feel, but only "sidecar" and "sieve" and "machine" came out. My oldest daughter, who was with me, lowered her head as she did not know whether to laugh or be scared. However, this was no joking matter. This was the moment I realized there was a severe problem. In my mind, I could feel the words a shirt, a shoe, a picture of a beach with sea and sand, a shoreline, seashells, a sink, a bar of soap, and the smile on my daughter's face, but these words were lost somewhere in between my brain and my mouth.

BLINK, CRASH, AND CONSEQUENCE

Life changes in the blink of an eye, yet the impact can last a lifetime.

— MARISSA MAYER

About seven weeks before, I was sitting in a parked car, waiting for my younger daughter to come out of Chipotle with burritos. I recall removing my seatbelt to reach for my phone as I saw a group of teenagers hurrying to their car parked behind me. Strangely, they were only wearing shorts and t-shirts with no coats on this cold, snowy, rain-mixed March night in 2016, but then I remembered that the high school talent show was running a dress rehearsal that night. My eyes met one of the boys, and his smile had a trace of guilt as he knew that if I were his mother, I would have told him to put on a coat. Moments later, I heard an engine roar and tires screech. The young driver did not realize that his tires had been frozen to the pavement with the wet snow and rain, and he over-compensated. I looked in the rearview mirror and saw his car quickly lurching out of control, hitting mine squarely on the bumper. My body took the impact, slamming my head on the side window before swinging back against the seat like an egg outside of its carton. Life slowed down at that point. I remember the crowd rushing out of the store, the police coming to assess the accident, giving them a statement, and how the snow gently fell on the car and pavement. Suddenly, it was all too much. The volume of everyday speech seemed to have reached maximum; the pavement spun, and I felt nauseous. We drove to the emergency room, where I was x-rayed, CAT-scanned, and MRI'ed. At this point, I felt lucky that nothing was broken or bleeding, but I had a definite haze coming over me as a disjointed reality of seeing, hearing, and doing was quickly setting in as I looked at the stack of papers that described what would become all too familiar to me over the next several years—the diagnosis of a concussion.

MONDAY'S CHALLENGE

It is not from the benevolence of the butcher, the brewer, or the baker that we expect our dinner, but from their regard for their own interest.

— ADAM SMITH

I went to the office on Monday because that was something I always did—work hard. I rationalized that it was only an accident, a bump on the back of the car, and I had taken it easy over the weekend. However, I felt sick within minutes. The commute, walking through the parking lot, and the harsh lights and noise of the office had a cumulative effect on me. My manager had no empathy for me as I told her of my accident. In retrospect, her reaction is a telling portrayal of Corporate America and how, once we walk through the office doors, the rules that govern humanity seem to take on a new dimension. She asked that I run a meeting with stakeholders and then go home if I was still not feeling well. I ran the meeting, not remembering much of what happened, and then left.

I did my best when I returned to the office a week later. At this point, I did not grasp the severity of the concussion or how my whole life had changed in a moment. I did not understand how a concussion was affecting not only the pace of my work but also my speech, cognitive processing, visual acuity, and how I accomplished daily life activities. However, these realizations were slowly becoming clear in frustrating ways, such as hitting spell check and realizing there were too many errors, not responding to questions at an appropriate pace, and being exhausted after work, to the point of doing nothing but sleep when I got home. By May, almost seventy days post-accident, this work-life pace was just too much for me, and my doctor placed me on short-term disability. During these weeks, my early mornings were productive, as I fell into a very focused routine of getting up and dressed and making the bed, but after that, the rest of the day would float away until I realized it was late afternoon and time for dinner. I did not realize how limited my life had become, as I did not have a reference point. However, when cooking became challenging and almost frightening, when I had trouble preparing simple meals, forgot to turn off the stove, and could not safely use sharp knives, I realized this pursuit was dangerous and needed to create better boundaries. After several weeks, I felt like I was falling deeper into a hole with no way out.

PRELUDE TO CHANGE

Life can only be understood backward, but it must be lived forward.

— SØREN KIERKEGAARD

Before the accident, my co-workers and friends may have considered me a driven, A-type personality, living a vibrant life with family, church, challenging work, and community activities. In the aftermath of the diagnosis, there were moments of anger, frustration, fear, and uncertainty about the future, and the sudden disruption to my life left me feeling vulnerable and overwhelmed. What was the most frustrating was that from the outside, there was nothing broken, so I appeared "normal" to anyone looking, but the way my brain was reacting to stimuli was so off from what was "normal" for me, and I could not find a way to get back to my former self.

One day, I remembered a program in which the host spoke about some neurological problems that he was having. His symptoms were similar to mine, and he spoke of a group of doctors in Dallas who had some groundbreaking therapies adapted from NASA for handling his challenges of walking and his inability to talk. So, I found their website and called. The woman on the phone explained what my neurologist never did about concussions and traumatic brain injuries and how the many symptoms can manifest. This conversation was the first glimmer of hope I had in the months since the accident. I finally had a reasonable explanation for my brain fog and other seemingly random symptoms, and to my relief, I was not alone. Within two weeks, I was on a plane to Dallas for ten days of intensive rehabilitative therapy and an updated diagnosis of traumatic brain injury as well as post-concussion syndrome. For the first time in a long time, my future did not seem clouded with uncertainty.

I tell this story not to elicit sympathy, as this narrative is familiar in our fast-paced world, but to show that life can change in a moment and present unexpected hurdles that seem insurmountable, testing our resilience and determination. However, instead of letting this major setback define me, I confronted it head-on with strategic risk-taking and unwavering perseverance. This excerpt is about taking a defining moment in your life and recognizing it as an opportunity for growth and self-discovery. Instead of surrendering to despair, I resolved to face these challenges with strategic risk principles, knowing that overcoming this adversity would lead to personal transformation and an unstoppable mindset.

THE IMPACT OF ADVERSITY

"The only way to handle life's challenges is by facing them."

— VIOLA DAVIS

Despite the uncertainties of my new lived reality, I recognized an opportunity for growth and self-discovery in my recovery. Adversity reveals our inner strengths and resilience, pushing us to confront our limitations and attempts to rise above them. So it was that moment of deciding to go to Dallas, rather than allowing myself to be defined by my circumstances, that I knew that I had chosen to be resolved and face these challenges with determination. While no one wants to experience adversity's challenges, it is an aspect of our human experience and presents an opportunity for growth and resilience. Adversity can shape us into unstoppable forces capable of overcoming any obstacle. This life-altering challenge forced me to reassess my priorities, values, and beliefs. In addition, I also received the powerful gifts of increased empathy and compassion as I gained a deeper understanding of the struggles faced by so many others, which forced me to rise above my circumstances and push past limitations to become a better version of myself.

I am not suggesting that overcoming adversity is easy, as the way forward may not be clear, and moving from where you are in a new direction can seem complex and uncertain, but it is possible with resilience, determination, and support from others around you. Each problem you overcome will strengthen your resilience and resolve, empowering you to face future challenges with additional confidence and courage. For me, overcoming adversity required a healthy dose of humility to be willing to learn from my mistakes, to adapt to my changing circumstances, and to persevere in the pursuit of the goal of regaining pieces of my former life. Looking back at this process, I believe I became stronger and wiser, which developed a new and unstoppable will than ever before.

One of the most powerful aspects of adversity I discovered was the ability to transform the many obstacles I faced into opportunities. The concussion and its cognitive hardship forced me to think outside the box, explore new possibilities, and adapt to changing circumstances. It reawakened my innovation, creativity, and resilience as I learned to persist and take opportunities as they appeared. One example of this was that I now had a chance to create profound change for myself and our society. Using this power as a catalyst for change, I am working to create a more just, equitable, and resilient world for all rather than for a few. Over time, I developed a new, unstoppable mindset on approaching challenges, and now I can look at problems with a growth mindset, trying to maintain a positive outlook and address the inevitable setbacks and struggles with a newfound determination. One way I achieved this was to celebrate even the smallest of wins, which gave me the encouragement and self-motivation I needed to keep moving forward. These wins created a sense of pride and built confidence and gratitude, empowering me to continue my journey with courage and determination.

THE RETURN TO ROUTINE

"Success is not final; failure is not fatal: It is the courage to continue that count."

— WINSTON CHURCHILL

I returned to the Dallas clinic in October for a repeat of testing, cognitive exercises, and intensive physical therapy, and a few months later, in January, ten months post-accident, I returned to work. I made this decision with great consideration and decided it was the best way to get back into a routine and from being isolated and not cognitively challenged at home. The first few weeks in the high-rise office building with a sea of cubicles, overhead fluorescent lighting, noise, and people were rough. Getting to my desk from the parking lot, up an elevator, and down the long hallways was almost insurmountable. I would try to work on the small project I was assigned but turning on the computer and checking emails was about the extent of my capability at that time. I often challenged myself to walk down the 200-foot hallways of the building, choosing a focal point and working on the walking techniques the Clinic taught me, but I was emotionally vulnerable at this point as I would need to take frequent breaks to readjust and continue forward. Another therapy I continued was using a touch screen to relate words to each other, starting with simple words and moving to more complex words and phrases. Even after a few minutes, these activities were mentally exhausting, and I was critical of myself from the outside, looking in, "How can you not know that peanut butter goes with jelly, or race aligns with a car?" Nevertheless, with this cognitive disability, these tasks were a struggle.

Despite my best efforts, there were many setbacks on my road to recovery. There were moments of frustration and disappointment when any progress seemed just out of reach.

However, I refused to let these obstacles define my journey. Instead, I forced myself to reframe them as learning experiences and used my skills as a project manager to see these situations as opportunities to change my approach and course-correct. Each setback created the courage to continue moving forward, logically knowing that persistence was how I would overcome this adversity. In addition, I spent much effort masking my cognitive challenges during project calls. However, I do not want to minimize the immense mental determination it takes to mask invisible cognitive challenges, as this way of getting through the workday is an everyday reality for many people in our organizations.

REACHING OUT FOR SUPPORT

In our vulnerability, there is courage, and in our willingness to ask for help, there is strength.

— BRENÉ BROWN

It is normal to want to give up during setbacks and feel discouraged. However, I found that true strength lies in persisting through adversity and moving forward even when the path seems uncertain. At this point, I did acknowledge the reality of my situation and that perhaps my life trajectory, whatever it was before my accident, was gone, and I found myself on an entirely new road. This life shift was not necessarily bad, but since it was out of my control and I would not return to my life as it was, I needed to come to terms with my new reality and do it quickly. Fortunately, I had good employee benefits, so I set up sessions with a social worker through my company's Employee Assistance Program (EAP).

With this work, I gradually curated an unstoppable mindset. I was determined and refused to be defined by my circumstances or constrained by the fear that frequently set in. Instead, I focused on the possibilities and created a sense of resilience. I believed that I had the power to reshape my destiny. With each physical or cognitive victory, my confidence grew, pushing me forward with renewed determination, and that true personal strength lies not in avoiding challenges but in facing them head-on with courage and flexibility.

However, the self-doubt held me back; the voice in my mind

whispered, "You are not good enough," or "You will never succeed." Nevertheless, overcoming self-doubt is an essential piece to cultivate an unstoppable mindset. I chose to shift from allowing negative thoughts to dictate my actions or inactions and challenge these thoughts with evidence of my past successes and wins. I spent countless hours reminding myself of times when I had overcome a challenge or achieved a goal, practicing self-compassion and replacing self-critical thoughts with affirmations of my worth and capabilities. By confronting this self-doubt head-on, I built confidence and cultivated a mindset of resilience and determination.

Believing in your will and ability to shape your destiny is fundamental to cultivating an unstoppable mindset. We cannot be bystanders in our lives, and we need to realize that it is incumbent only on ourselves to make the choices and take the actions that lead us closer to our goals by taking ownership of our journey and embracing the power of personal choice. I established clear goals and planned to achieve them with this internal work. I did this by breaking down the larger goals into manageable steps and taking consistent and sustained action toward achieving them. In the end, I was able to steer my life in a new and exciting direction that was not even on my radar before the accident. I took control of my destiny, refused to be limited by circumstances beyond my control, and created a mindset of empowerment and resilience.

EMBRACING CHANGE

In the midst of chaos, there is also opportunity.

— SUN TZU

Our human experience is a journey filled with uncertainties and risks. Every decision, whether big or small, involves an element of risk. However, navigating these risks determines our success and shapes our future. Embracing strategic risk-taking involves making informed decisions that push us out of our familiar territory to propel us toward our goals. As an Organizational Change Consultant, I consider strategic risk to evaluate different approaches to gauge exposures within an acceptable tolerance level. While some risks may lead to failure or setbacks, others may result in success and growth. The issue is to assess the potential risks and rewards, weigh them carefully, and make decisions that align with your goals and values.

Strategic risk-taking is not about being reckless or impulsive. It involves making calculated decisions that have the potential to produce positive outcomes and perhaps step out of our comfort zones to embrace uncertainty to pursue growth and success. It involves being proactive rather than reactive and taking the initiative to create opportunities for ourselves rather than waiting for them to come our way.

One of the critical aspects of strategic risk-taking is being open to exploring alternate paths and considering options beyond the obvious. Often, the most rewarding opportunities lie outside our comfort zones, and we must be brave enough to examine them. Furthermore, by trying new approaches, venturing into new industries, or pursuing unconventional ideas, we can open ourselves to new experiences and opportunities for growth. Therefore, although these paths involve uncertainty and risk, they offer great discoveries and innovation potential.

EXPLORING ALTERNATIVES

> Nature itself is the best physician.
>
> — HIPPOCRATES

Taking strategic risks became an instrumental part of my journey to live a new kind of life with post-concussion syndrome. I realized that staying within my comfort zone only limited my potential for progress. Therefore, I embarked on a path of exploration, seeking alternative therapies and treatments. Each decision to try something new was a calculated risk, but I believed it could lead to break-throughs in my recovery. By embracing the uncertainty and venturing into uncomfortable territory, I discovered the values of resilience and strength I had forgotten were in me and discovered potential remedies beyond the traditional Western medical approaches. From acupuncture and chiropractic care to mindfulness, energy meditation, and supplements, I left no stone unturned in my pursuit of healing. In addition, I was creating a new unstoppable mindset by embracing growth and learning as essential components of my personal development. I sought opportunities for learning and development through formal education, skill-building workshops, and experiences where I could thrive in the face of my challenges.

Fast forward to 2021, I was distressed that corporations were not adequately prepared to accommodate employees with cognitive differences. I was fascinated by organizational change concepts in the post-COVID hybrid work environment and was invited to join a doctoral program at USC to study these issues. At the start of my research into mental health, bias, and neurodivergence, I kept bumping up against my own new lived experience, which reminded me of how much my life had changed. However, I found that this new cognitive change in how my mind worked had created an almost superpower effect for sustained research and the ability to empathize with social justice issues as never before. One of my research findings was that for many neurodivergents, their challenges are mostly invisible until they are not; in my case, they are very apparent when they do show up. As a result, I have learned from my experience that I must find different accommodations. One of the combinations I have been working with is taking advantage of the technology and not putting my stigma or bias against it with self-talk of "I do not need that. I can do it just as well." With technology and AI tools, I found that I can produce much more content in less time and in a more organized way, which has been a huge win and produces a sense of achievement.

TACKLING NEURODIVERGENT CHALLENGES IN THE WORKPLACE

For I am about to do something new. See, I have already begun! Do you not see it? I will make a pathway through the wilderness. I will create rivers in the dry wasteland.

— ISAIAH 43:19 NLT

In my research, I look at how corporations can successfully hire and retain neurodivergents in their workforces. While many companies have excellent programs, others are struggling to develop ways to address this growing population. In 2019, the CDC estimated that the number of ADHD/ADD students graduating into the workforce is estimated to be 500,000 per year. This figure does not include many of the other conditions that are also considered neurodivergent, such as PTSD, Tourette's Syndrome, the autism spectrum, anxiety, depression, dyslexia, or acquired brain injury. In my study, I found that the success of neurodivergents in the workplace is a direct result of executive-level leadership building a culture of inclusion and belonging within the organization. My focus on the hiring funnel found that many neurodivergents are either underemployed or unemployed because they cannot manage the corporate workplace environments, and the behavioral interview styles still in use. I recall my early post-accident days in my workplace, where I struggled with the office environment and its demands. With advancements in this science, it is no longer acceptable for workplaces to employ hiring practices based on thirty-year-old paradigms. With the sheer number of neurodivergents coming into today's workforce, we have to do better.

EMBRACING STRATEGIC VENTURES

The only strategy that is guaranteed to fail is not taking risks.

— MARK ZUCKERBERG

Many people do not take strategic risks because of the potential for failure, which is a genuine concern. However, failure is an inevitable part of being human. Early in this journey, I decided that by embracing my failures and reframing them as a natural part of the learning process, I could overcome my fear of taking strategic risks and confidently pursue my goals.

Adopting a strategic risk-taking mindset also requires resilience and adaptability, as it is essential to be prepared for setbacks and develop the resilience to bounce back from them, navigating the uncertainties of life with courage. One way I achieved this was to build a supportive network of peers and colleagues who encouraged and motivated me to keep pushing forward when facing struggles. Ultimately, embracing strategic risk-taking requires taking action and forward momentum despite uncertainty and doubt, making difficult decisions, taking calculated risks, and jumping feet-first into the unknown. Only when we are at that point of no return can we recognize and seize the opportunities when they arise, unlocking our full potential and achieving success beyond our wildest dreams.

DISRUPTING OBSOLETE CORPORATE NORMS

Change begins when we dare to challenge the status quo and break free from the limitations of old paradigms.

— UNKNOWN

As we continue to learn about the spectrum of normal human cognitive fluidity and creativity, it becomes clear that accepting neurodiversity is essential to fostering inclusivity, driving innovation and progress in our organizations and communities, and paving the way for a more dynamic and innovative future. In addition, embracing neurodiversity can foster a more inclusive and supportive work environment. By creating a culture that values and celebrates neurodiversity, companies can create a sense of belonging for all employees, benefiting neurodivergent team members and enhancing the overall morale and productivity of the entire organization. Of course, transitioning to this inclusive culture requires a concerted effort from both the leadership and employees, which can involve implementing training programs to raise awareness about neurodiversity, providing accommodations and support services for neurodivergent individuals, and fostering a culture of open-mindedness and acceptance. By actively championing diversity and inclusion, companies can create a workplace where all employees feel valued and empowered to contribute their unique talents and perspectives.

Breaking down the old corporate paradigms of groupthink and narrow definitions of "good fit" employees is essential for unlocking the full potential of neurodiversity in the workplace. As a neurodivergent individual who has experienced the transformative power of embracing diversity firsthand, I believe the future belongs to companies that dare to challenge the status quo and embrace the human cognitive spectrum. It is time to reimagine what being a team player means and pave the way for a more inclusive and innovative future. By prioritizing neurodiversity in the workplace, companies can challenge these systemic inequalities and create opportunities for individuals who have been traditionally overlooked or marginalized. In essence, embracing neurodiversity is a good business decision and a moral imperative that our shareholders, communities, and markets demand, which speaks to our shared commitment to justice and equity.

RECOGNIZING MY PURPOSE AS INTENTIONAL, NOT CHANCE

The two most important days in your life are the day you are born, and the day you find out why.

— MARK TWAIN

I was fortunate to be able to find a way forward in which my post-concussion syndrome could not label or defeat me. I did this by accepting and embracing that my brain now works differently. Furthermore, despite the challenges and triumphs, I defied the odds by embracing strategic risk-taking, persisting in the face of setbacks, and cultivating an unstoppable mindset. With this narrative, it is clear that I leveraged all the skills and abilities I learned and cultivated throughout my life. Through perseverance and strategic risk, all the pieces came together through the fogginess of my mind to create my new life.

Furthermore, I emerged as a stronger and better version of my former self. My journey exemplifies the power of resilience and determination in overcoming adversity and achieving personal growth. Through it all, I learned that no obstacle is insurmountable when faced with courage and unwavering drive, and you, too, can shape your destiny and create the life you desire. With an unstoppable mindset, there is no limit to what you can achieve. I hope you can embrace life with courage and conviction and never stop pursuing your dreams.

Learn more about Dr. Nancy Morehouse here:

ABOUT DR. NANCY MOREHOUSE

Dr. Nancy Morehouse is a distinguished author and thought leader in organizational change, leadership development, and risk management. With a Doctorate in Organizational Change and Leadership from the University of Southern California and a Certification in AI for Business Growth from Northwestern University, Nancy helps businesses navigate the complexities of the post-COVID corporate landscape.

Her publications and speaking engagements offer invaluable insights into effective leadership, organizational resilience, and strategic change initiatives.

Outside of her professional endeavors, Nancy is an avid traveler and amateur photographer, finding inspiration in the beauty of diverse cultures and landscapes. She resides in the Midwest with her family and Golden Retriever, Bowdoin, finding joy in life's simple pleasures and the pursuit of knowledge.

Connect with her to explore her thought-provoking publications and engage in conversations about equity, leadership, organizational change, and how to leverage Artificial Intelligence and risk management to increase business growth.

Website: *www.linkedin.com/in/nancymorehouse*

12

COLONEL VANESSA MOSES

Twenty years old, a sophomore in college and pregnant. I had no idea what I was going to do. If you are a believer of a higher power, then I suggest you dial into that when times get tough. I prayed for strength... "Lord, just get me through this." I knew I had the brain power... but what was ahead, I did not think I could endure. Having a baby at 21 years old is scary as hell! I was basically a teenager +4 years, my maturity level was not yet of an adult. I still wanted to "live out loud." I was out-going, loved to party... partake in liquid spirits and other activities that gets your juices flowing. But all of that came to a screeching halt when I delivered the most beautiful baby girl I had ever seen. My granddaddy (resting in heaven) would tell me, I took a mold of my face and put it on hers. Every time I looked down at her sweet face with her big smile, I knew I had to do something different. I did not know what... I just knew I had to change. This was when I threw my life into a completely different direction. All the partying and good times seem to not be as important. Now don't get me wrong, I still loved my liquid spirits and shaking a leg from time to time, but now someone else is depending on me to ensure they get (not just me) a head start on life. And when that challenge set in... it was on! I love a good challenge, still to this very day!

At the time I was an E-3 in the Army Reserves, 312th Field Hospital, while attending North Carolina Agricultural & Technical State University. Even though I was "doing my thang," I had friends right there with me through it all. From the 2am - 6am parties to crying with me because I was in disbelief that I was pregnant, those same friends supported me then and they still do today. I had to drop out of college for a couple of reasons. 1) I was pregnant with no means of supporting myself, so I went back home. 2) I had to get my shit together. But I knew I needed the Matriarch! The woman who gave me life and still gives me life every single day. My mom and dad supported me DAY ONE! Both were always there no matter how hard it got... they pushed to ensure I did NOT give up. They would NOT let me. My dad would tell me..." you are so smart, have the baby, we will keep her, you just need to finish school." They believed in me when I did not believe in myself. That gave me the strength I needed.

I served as a Combat Medic for a little over 3 years, then I went off to complete an additional technical school to become a 91C, Licensed Practical Nurse (LPN), while my daughter was only 1 years old. This opportunity gave me the bridge I needed to get back on track to finish my bachelor's degree in nursing (BSN). I finished the Army's 91C course in the summer of 1996, challenged the LPN exam and passed. That fall I re-enrolled back into school to become a Registered Nurse. I chose Winston Salem State University. My LPN transcript was evaluated, and they gave me credit towards 2 courses that were typically taught in the summer. Still in the Army reserves, now a full-time college student, and working at a nursing home to provide for myself. My parents honored their promise, while I attended college and worked, they kept and raised my daughter. I sent money home to assist with raising her and went home whenever I could. Because of this decision, there were several individuals extremely judgmental in my choice to serve, go to school and ensure my daughter had a stable life while I tried to pull my life together.

Thankfully my parents were like me, we didn't give a damn what people thought.

Serving in the Army reserves taught and showed me things I loved and other things, well let's just call them challenges. The experience I gained was bar none. The ruggedness of training, the in-your-face bootcamp and tech school... I could not get enough of. I loved it. Even now, I love it when folks are direct in their conversation.

1998, I graduated with my BSN; I could not have been prouder of myself. Still in the reserves, but by this time I changed jobs. Now working at a Pediatric Rehab Hospital, bartending, and waiting tables; there is decent money to be made in the restaurant industry. One night my tips were so good, I paid for summer school IN FULL. It was easy fast money, but legal. After obtaining my RN license I searched for other jobs, my goal was to become a Labor and Delivery nurse, so I kept my focus there. Despite there not being any availability, the manager interviewing gave me a position in the High-Risk Antepartum department. This position allowed me to learn and get closer to Labor and Delivery with the ability to "float" to other units when requested. I often get fidgety and want to try something new. With my RN, BSN, I started seeing posters about Air Force (AF) Flight Nursing and fell instantly IN-LOVE! I began chatting with a recruiter to see how to start the process. Initially, I wanted to commission in the AF Reserves, but the more the recruiter talked and enticed me, the more I wanted to go Active Duty! Yes, they GOT ME! There was just one thing, I could not do Flight Nursing initially on Active Duty, but the recruiter did say, "you can do Labor and Delivery on your first assignment"! I was hooked! I get to commission and do a job I have always wanted... SOLD!

It was 2000, and "off I go into the wild blue yonder." I started my Air Force career. I attended Commissioned Officers Training that summer. It was a bit challenging, but absolutely nothing like Army boot camp. I had a private billeting/hotel room, and maid service! From being enlisted to becoming an officer, things were surely different on this side. In Army boot camp, I slept in a bunk bed with about 40-50 other women in a large bay area, along with community showers. Yes, life from enlisted to officer was completely different. But I lived and loved them both.

I then head to my first assignment Malcom Grow Medical Center, Andrews Air Force Base, which is honestly why I think I am still serving today. I worked with an amazing group of diverse individuals. It was simply a melting pot of nationalities! On our rough day/nights, we sat in the hallway on the floor and talked. Openly discussing what happened. This was therapeutic for all of us. We were not just a team; we were a family. And I have embodied this camaraderie throughout my career. We would leave our night shift and head to iHop to get our "eat on." I was a 2Lt (butter bar) living large, now in the city with a group of people who loved living out loud too. My daughter was back with me, and I am slowly but surely pulling myself together nicely. She had an old soul, engaging in conversations with adults easily. She could be found at the hospital with me, at one of my co-worker's houses who also had kids or playing sports. She was super independent and smart as hell!

2003, my daughter and I head off to our first overseas assignment. We flew into Luxembourg and were picked up by my sponsor for 52d Medical Group Bitburg Air Base Annex/Spangdahlem. It was a small hospital where I continued to do Labor and Delivery, but also had the opportunity to work Medical-Surgical Nursing, Same-Day Surgery, and Emergency Room (ER) but it was more like an Urgent Care. So, I did! I learned and worked every area in the hospital and loved it. Once again, I am embedded with a team with some challenges in the beginning, but after about 6 months this team becomes family. Because I worked in the ER, when my daughter was injured at a sports event, I could check her in do the assessment and the doctor would then see her. There was zero wait for us. One of the nurses on the floor could sew, she made all my daughters costumes for dance. When I was the team mom for her sports team, I did one of the banquets at the hospital. We had a small picnic area in the back, the staff assisted decorating the hospital from the front to the back so everyone would know where to go. All enjoyed the food while the coaches did their presentations. There was even a time I contemplated getting out of the military and my daughter stated, "who is going to take care of our medical." She was only 9 years old at the time, but knew we had no problems getting in to see a doctor. I still chuckle about that today.

2006, I am off and ready for my next challenge! And it is exactly what I wanted. FLIGHT NURSING! I head to flight nursing school, survival school and water survival to ultimately land at Pope AFB, North Carolina assigned to the mighty 43d Aeromedical Evacuation Squadron. This assignment is where my operational mindset took shape. The training this unit prides itself in, could not be beat. We took training seriously. Everyone in this unit was direct and no-nonsense! Our deployment tempo was high, but we all did not hesitate to go out the door when called. We were on a 1:1 dwell. That meant Deploy 4 months, Home 4 months, Deploy 4 months and the cycled continued. Our unit's patch stated "Always the First" ... and that was true. If something happened in the world, our unit was called. Most of us kept bags partially packed because sometimes we were on 6 ring standbys. That meant, you need to answer your phone within 6 rings because most likely you were headed to go somewhere to support something. We had amazing teamwork and yes family like ties. Don't try and fight any one in the 43d, if so, you just bought yourself a beat down. I remember having to stand in between my members and members of another unit, while deployed to Germany. Mind you, we probably had a bit too much to drink. But remember I lived in Germany before deploying there. And drinking is like a sport... and many learn how to play very well. When we got back to the hotel, we all chuckled. One of my teammates called a C-17 pilot a glorified bus driver. They were getting ready to tear the club up... until I jumped in, putting my hands out (I am dressed up a bit with high heels on) to stop the interactions. But that didn't stop me. I love that unit and the people. They were always ready to go, wherever, whenever. Our unit was deactivated a few years ago and many of us keep in touch. There is nothing like going to combat with someone then having the ability to come back home with those same folks, some didn't get that opportunity. Those bonds we built... unbreakable. Freedom is not Free, Never Was, Never Will Be! I deployed (>120 days) 4 times and supported (<30 days) 6 contingency operations. Honestly, if I had to do it all over again... I would! In a nano second!

2011, I get what I call my first high profile job. I am the Director of the Flight Nurse Course United States Air Force School of Aerospace Medicine. That rolls off your tongue nicely, right! Here is yet another job I fell in love with, and I didn't even want to go. I was a non-volunteer. I went as an instructor, but quickly moved into the Director's position. I had a direct impact on the future of the career field that brought me in the Air Force. Training Active-Duty Air Force, Guard, Reserve... a few Army, Navy, and partner nation attendees, how can anything compare to that? I remember crying at the last graduation, while I pinned their wings on for the last time. An emotional event for sure.

2014, just when I think I can't get another great position, I am Development Team selected to serve as the Senior Nurse at the Army/Air Force clinic on Ft. Bragg. Here was an opportunity for me to hone in on my communication skills with the Army. Because I was prior Army, this came quite easy for me. We had several leaders come through, and I remember one speaking to the group (Army & Air Force Leadership) and asked, "why does this joint environment work?" One of the Army personnel pointed at me and stated, "she has an Air Force uniform on, but she is still pretty much Army."

2016, I am again Development Team selected again, this time competitively for a leadership fellowship. I head to Texas as the 59 Medical Wing Nurse Executive Fellow! I was shocked! What an opportunity? I was able to shadow several senior leaders and organizations, attend Evidence Based Practice Classes, and a Continuous Process Improvement Course. I was also a guest speaker to several nursing courses on the campus of METC (Military Education

Training Center). I met so many influential personnel, I am connected to today. As my fellowship comes to an end, senior leaders stand ready to assist in my next opportunity. There were some who wanted me to take another clinic position, which I did not want because I had just left the clinic prior to taking my fellowship.

While shadowing the assignments officers at AFPC (Air Force Personnel Center), I simply asked what 1-year jobs were available, because I knew I wanted to compete for Squadron Command first chance. The Assignment Officer (AO) stated, you will be an O-5 so no need in looking at O-4 positions. There were no positions in Turkey or Korea for an O-5. But there was one in a deployed location, so the AO put me down for the Chief, Aeromedical Evacuation (AE) Control Team. I had at least 2 senior leaders advocating for me to get that position. And yes, I was selected for the position to serve 1 year in a deployed location. I attended the AOCIQT (Air Operations Center Initial Qualification Training) getting my SEI (Special Education Identifier). After I arrived on-sight, I was trained by one of the savviest AE gurus I knew. I felt blessed but was humbled quickly when I stepped into this environment that was super-fast paced. I watched my controllers as they navigated the system, so I attached myself to them. They knew the job and within 45 days I had all things locked in too! The team set me up for ultimate success!

We had amazing leadership allowing us to take necessary risk to ensure the missions went well if not flawless. The AE team worked effortlessly with our line of the AF partners. Teamwork makes the dreamwork. This position solidified my operational expertise. While in that position, I was named the AMD (Air Mobility Division) Officer of the Year. One of the new fellows was in charge of the AFMS (Air Force Medical Service) Nurse Corp Face book page, requested my bio and a picture. She proudly posted the announcement of my award, gaining AF wide attention.

Of course, I competed for squadron command first chance. Unfortunately, I was not selected. After, I received feedback on why I was not, I was baffled at the response. However, I was a candidate on the Chief Nurse list and beyond ecstatic when I was selected to serve in Okinawa Japan, 18th Aeromedical Evacuation Squadron, Kadena Air Base. Another dream job on a tropical island! Literally, the drive to the office is an ocean view. The mission was busy. Flyers often gone for weeks at a time albeit in Hawaii, Guam, Korea, and other great locations. There were rarely any complaints simply because going to the beach was a daily outlet. Listening to the ocean brought all peace. But we did endure typhoon evacs! Planes and crews whisked away off the island! It still was a good time. Then COVID hits, which made things a bit more challenging. Most everything closed down! All did what worked for them to maintain sanity. By the time I was off for my next adventure the beaches were open, but most places were still closed. For my going away we headed to the beach, drank Margaritas and STRONGS to just hung out. Then all of sudden the weather just flips, and dark clouds roll in quickly. We all gathered under a gazebo as "baby" typhoon rolls in. It is pouring rain... somebody had their speakers, so music was playing. One of the nurses shows up with my going away gift. She states, "let's talk about Moses." She says these super sweet things... and passes it to the next and then the next, with everyone saying a few words about me. Eventually making it around to everyone, even a few strangers made comments just from meeting me that night. By the time the gift made its way to me, I was in full blown "ugly" crying mode! I pulled it together and gave my speech. When I finished one of the other nurses... yells "Moses go run around in a circle in the rain?" Keep in mind... it was still pouring, but I ran out there and spun around in a circle! I was soaked! Another nurse stated, "I live close, just come over to dry off." She gave me clothes to change into... and then put my clothes in the dryer. Best going away ever!

2020, I was selected for my first Squadron Command. Nervous and frankly terrified upon my arrival. My personality is a bit strong having served in the Army and as a flight nurse with combat experience, I wasn't quite sure how I would be received back in the hospital. I was immediately put at ease, when the two officers taking care of my ceremony began to chat with me. I openly stated my concerns, one stated ma'am "I am prior enlisted security forces," the other stated "I am prior enlisted Navy." My eyes begin to swell with tears, that's when I knew... it was meant to be.

I was taking Command as the 52d Medical Operational Squadron Commander in the 52d Medical Group, where the leadership all around was supportive. We did our best to ensure positive outcomes on all things. What I loved the most was the honesty all came to the table with. It was no secret if someone did not like something, they voiced it. But what we did was get on the same page, if that meant a bit of a debate then so be it. We still left the room in agreeance! All commanders should experience something like this, this environment guaranteed us all success. But the trust started with my right hand, my Senior Enlisted (SEL)! We were on the same page majority of the time, if not we worked to get there quickly. My SEL is one of the reasons I was so successful. We had candid conversations frequently. He had no problems letting me know if he disagreed. I appreciated it because having a different perspective is what you need to make a sound decision. We wanted to ensure we were doing what was best for the entire team. And we did! This experience is the reason why I am competing for Medical Group Command. I am not saying it was perfect! But it was damn good!

2022, I was selected for Colonel! I cried like a baby! Goal Met! I worked hard! Did the hard jobs! Made the sacrifices! It was well earned! But this is where the 'Colonel's Group' decides your next job. With the help from some senior leaders who knew me and my work ethics... and the grace of God! I was selected to serve in the ULTI-MATE Aeromedical Evacuation job! I was the next 86th Aeromedical Evacuation (AE) Squadron Commander! When I tell you, I screamed and cried!! This was it! This was the DREAM JOB! This was pinnacle for me! My 5th assignment in a specialty I absolutely love, at a time when the ops tempo is high, there was nothing that could top this! Leading the people in an operational environment is my strong suit... and I came in wanting to make necessary change the AE enterprise. I rarely take no for an answer because I honestly feel there is ALWAYS a way to yes.

I analyzed my team. Learned their strengths and weaknesses as well as my own. I hired folks that closed the gaps on my weaknesses. But, if there was dead weight, I dropped it. Teams depends on leaders to ensure the mission moves forward, taking care of people and cutting through the red tape. Putting the people first will get you there every time. Once you master, or at least learn how to take care of people well... you will see those same people easily take care of the mission.

The 86 AES is comprised of powerhouses and total bad asses! We are a fast-paced operational unit, embracing innovation, changing the enterprise, making history... and standing ready to cut through any and all red tape. These members are fearless! And ready for combat medicine! Led by me... with superior top cover leadership!

My career has been fast-moving, and I have loved it! Things have always remained interesting. But with all of this... I still live completely "out loud"! Shopping, eating, enjoying liquid spirits, and traveling... the lifestyle of a true DIVA! You may see me in the mall, in the bar or maybe even in Ibiza! I am the same person! Serving and being... authentically me.

But I have learned to disconnect from it all. I prioritize my Mental Health over all things! No one is going to take better care of me... than me! I have often heard..." you are selfish!" My response now is ... "AND?" My life... and I am living it my way.

ABOUT COLONEL VANESSA MOSES

Colonel Moses, from Fayetteville, North Carolina, is a resilient and purposeful individual. She has navigated through challenges with unwavering determination, emerging stronger with each obstacle overcome. Fueling her journey is a deep-seated love for being true to herself, which she channels into works of inspiration, inviting others to explore the depths of their own imagination and embrace the power of storytelling. Vanessa embarked on a lifelong quest for intellectual growth and enlightenment, dedicated to expanding the boundaries of understanding and gaining insights that shaped her contributions to society.

Throughout her military journey, Vanessa has made significant contributions to her field of expertise, demonstrating a deep commitment to making a positive difference in the lives of others. Vanessa celebrates cultural exchange and fosters understanding and empathy across divides, creating spaces where individuals from all walks of life feel seen, heard, and valued. Through her resilience and compassion, Vanessa serves as an inspiring example of what it means to embrace authenticity and make a difference in the world. Vanessa continues to inspire others to push the boundaries of possibility, inviting them on a journey of discovery, growth, and transformation.

13
DR. ALISHA SMITH

*I*t's three o'clock in the morning and I'm wide awake. Staring at the ceiling in the dark, wondering "how did I get here?" I'm in a twin bed in the middle of someone's living room; everything I own is in my car outside; I have no place to call home. This isn't supposed to happen to someone like me... This can't be my life! I have three jobs, I'm a full-time college student, and I'm in the Air Force National Guard. I work hard, I'm nice to everyone. Meanwhile, I move through the world every day, and no one knows that I am suffering in silence. I can't even count the number of times I have thought of how easy it would be to just drive off a cliff and end it all.

I was born to a young teenage mom who sacrificed everything for me. It wasn't until I was older and wiser that I realized how hard my mother struggled to give me a "normal" life and childhood. I never knew I didn't have everything because no matter what it was, she provided. We essentially grew up together and that has been the foundation of the amazingly close bond we share today.

I grew up as a military brat because my dad was in the Army. I went to four different high schools my senior year alone and graduated with people I had known for about four months, so to say we moved a lot is an understatement. I completed my first two years of college at home and then moved off on my own because my parents got another assignment. Little did I know the next several years of my life would be filled with turmoil, depression, heartbreak, and struggle.

I was like any "normal" college student. I wanted to be on my own, have fun with my friends, and get my degree so that I could be a productive member of society. I wasn't the kid with the college fund —my parents couldn't afford that. So, I took out loans, got every credit card they would approve me for, and quickly realized this was not going to be easy. I had already moved into my first roach-infested apartment, and later decided it would be "easier" with a roommate. That decision ended up with an eviction notice and no way to pay for my upcoming classes.

At this point, I was about two weeks from my classes being dropped, I was too afraid to tell my parents because I knew they would worry, and I saw a commercial... "Come join the Oklahoma Air National Guard and we will give you a 100% tuition waiver!" That was my next adventure! I called my parents, told them I was enlisting and my dad's response, "pick the job with the longest technical training... It will help you be more marketable." Exactly three days before I was kicked out of school, my tuition was paid, and I was on my way to becoming an aircraft maintenance technician in the Air National Guard.

I never aspired to joining the military; it was always just a means to an end. I didn't give much thought to it being a career, and I really didn't like my job. I was one of two females in the unit, my supervisor and I, and it was certainly not easy being in a maintenance world of sexism. Looking back, I believe this was the start of me feeling like I always had to be better than everyone else. My best was never going to be enough, so I had to be an overachiever, constantly proving myself. This sentiment played out in my twenty-eight-year career in the military and while it brought me much success, it brought me equally the amount of heart ache, broken relationships, and pain.

Before finishing college, I found myself married young and for all the wrong reasons. I acknowledge that I needed a way out. A way out of the life I was living and a promise of a better opportunity. I quickly learned there is truth in the adage "hurt people hurt people." Five years into the marriage, I was a commissioned officer in the Air Force as a Hospital Administrator. From the outside looking in, I had the perfect life. I was winning all the awards at work, constantly being recognized by my leaders, but my life was falling apart at home. I was spending more and more time at work because it was the only thing I was good at.

I continued to be great at work, learning my craft, being a valuable team member. I went on to break barriers, make history with my promotions, and was selected to lead at multiple levels, serving some of the greatest men and women in our Armed Forces. While I am beyond proud of my professional accomplishments, I recognize that it all came at a great toll to my personal life. My marriage ended after twelve years and there were many days where I felt like I wasn't good enough—not at work... not at home... not at being ME!

Despite it all, I continued to work hard, pursue my education, and set the best example I could as I raise a daughter who inevitably was watching my every move. A blind date led me to my soul mate, who has allowed me the space to be 100% my authentic self. He has supported me through it all, and picked up the pieces when my heart was broken. The trials and struggles, coupled with completing a successful twenty-eight years in the Air Force, have taught me two valuable lessons: The power of service to others and building relationships is immeasurable, both personal and professional, are more important than anything else. Throughout this journey of service and building relationships, I've learned leadership, influence, networking, and collaboration are critical components to success. Of these, I believe leadership is most important because how you lead, personally and professionally, is the foundation of how you live your life.

There are many ways to define leadership. I simply define it as the ability to influence an individual or group to achieve a common goal or purpose. My leadership journey was definitely sharpened in the military; however, I have always believed that I would lead in some capacity, not because I thought I was that good, mainly because I believe leadership is service. Leaders GET to serve those they lead, they GET to remove barriers and they GET to inspire, and motivate, and unite people.

Admittedly, leadership has not always come easy for me. I learned some powerful, yet painful leadership lessons along the way. In fact, my most valuable lessons came from being subordinate to some leaders with very toxic traits. Little did they know I was taking notes, and they were reinforcing what I knew I didn't want to be as a leader, and at the same time, sharpening my leadership and communication skills so I could be that much better.

One of my most valuable leadership lessons came from a boss I will call "Mr. Do-It-Like-Me." He *earned* that name honestly! He was the kind of boss who liked to tell you what he wanted you to do, watch you do it, and then continue to change the intent the more you worked the project. Working for him was literally like nailing Jell-o to the wall. Nothing was good enough. He would task me with a project, I would turn it in, and after so many iterations of him making changes to the changes, I would just give up.

There were many days that I would be in tears because I worked so hard on something only for him to mark it all up with a red pen. In hindsight, I know that he just liked things a certain way, but in the moment what he conditioned me to do is submit a poor product because he was going to change it into what he wanted anyway, so why should I work so hard. That is a very dangerous mentality, and I knew that I couldn't fall into that trap because I have never been mediocre. I call this lesson "Let people be who they are."

As leaders grow in their scope and responsibility, there are just not enough hours in the day to do everything, read everything, or change and correct everything. Leaders are surrounded with talented teams of people who genuinely want to work and want to do the right thing. I remember exactly how Mr. Perfect made me feel every time he sent something back to me for corrections. I got more and more frustrated, more and more disheartened, and I remember feeling like he didn't want MY input; he just wanted a mini him.

I decided to never be THAT leader. My role is to define the end state and give people the time, space, and support to be innovative and solve problems. Although it was a very difficult lesson, I realized that if you just let people be who they are, they will surprise you with greatness. It will not be what you would have done, but just because it's different doesn't make it wrong, it's just different. Additionally, allowing people to be themselves creates buy-in to the shared goal and they become invested in the success of the team, thus working harder. Finally, they feel like they have the support of the leader and know that the leader cares about their worth to the team.

My next lesson came from "Mr. Oblivious." He was the type of leader who thought it was perfectly fine to say whatever was on his mind if he prefaced it with, "let's just talk." Mr. Ignorant had a pattern of discriminatory behavior toward women and especially minority women. I worked for Mr. Oblivious for about two years and was subjected to subtle and blatant discrimination. During one interaction, he wanted to "remind" me that I didn't get selected for my commission in the Air Force based on my merit. He told me that I was only selected because there was a quota for minorities that needed to be met and senior leaders had decided they needed to keep a few of "us" around so we can fill key positions in the Air Force Medical Service later.

I was appalled at his leadership and angry that we allowed these kinds of leaders to have influence over Airmen in our military. Mr. Oblivious taught me the value of diversity on a team. I wasn't the only person he discriminated against, but I noticed how we all banded together and excelled as a team, despite his ignorance.

Having led several diverse teams myself, I have learned that diversity of thought, background, and experiences make a team stronger because you have the gift of varying perspectives. It is incumbent upon a leader to ensure all members of a team feel valued and HEARD because their perspective contributes to the success of the team.

Mr. Do-It-Like-Me and Mr. Oblivious are two of the many "characters" responsible for my leadership lessons. I've learned the best leaders understand leadership is a privilege because you GET to serve those you lead, and only the humblest leaders can handle that burden of responsibility. Leaders are also inspiring and motivate people to be and do their best. I have never been the smartest person in a room, by far, but I know God has blessed me with the ability to see the best in people and inspire them to push themselves beyond their limits.

Dr. Maya Angelou had it right when she said, "I've learned that people will forget what you said, people will forget what you did, but people will never forget how you made them feel."

Humans are emotional beings, and we operate on feelings and connections. I have encountered so many people over the years and even though I may not remember every interaction, if it meant something to them, they remember.

One of my favorite bosses, "Mr. Personality," helped drive that lesson home. He was a very powerful leader, and he was always so busy, but he made time for people. No matter what he was doing or where he was, if he was talking to you, he had this way of making you feel like you were the only person in the room. I called him the politician. I had the pleasure of watching him in action for a year and I learned to understand the power of connecting with people. Not just interacting but connecting on a level that is meaningful to them... serving them in the capacity they need at that time.

I consider myself to come from very humble beginnings. My hope has always been that someone could see me and all that I have worked hard to achieve and that would inspire them to do the same.

I have found that most times, people just need someone to believe in them, offer them an encouraging word, and share an experience with them. We all need someone to pick us up and say, "Don't quit, you got this!"

None of us can make it through this life alone and that is why the power of networking and building relationships is so important. If you ask any successful person, they could list at least five people who were a part of their circle that helped them achieve success. It goes back to having a diverse team of individuals around you who will offer you varying perspectives and not always tell you what you want to hear. We need diversity both personally and professionally.

I intentionally seek out people who are different from me, in thought, gender, race, etc., who challenge me to think differently. It is uncomfortable, but I always say if you are not stretched, you don't grow. A great illustration is a rubber band. If you just put it down, it retains its shape, but if you pull on it in every direction, you will see that it is bigger when you put it down because of the tension in stretching it out of shape. Your relationships should stretch you to be bigger and better than you were.

Equally as important as networking is mentorship and collaboration. As we learn things along the way, we should share those lessons and always look for ways to prepare those coming behind us. It's how we succeed together. Mentorship is one of my favorite things to do. I always tell people that I am as transparent as I can possibly be, in my success and my shortcomings because I wish someone would have shared some of these things with me. I wish someone would have told me that I could have great success, but it would come at a cost and sacrifice to my personal life. That it would cost me a marriage, and time with my daughter. That sometimes, it's just plain hard!

No one expects you to be the smartest person in the room. Quite frankly, if you are the smartest person, then you are in the wrong room. Collaboration is the key to successful partnerships. For me, this applies personally and professionally. It is critical to recognize your gaps and gravitate toward people who compliment your strengths and fill your gaps. Again, no one makes it alone, and we are better when we work together to create meaningful relationships.

As I reflect on my life and career, I realize everything comes at a cost. I went from being a mediocre student to being a homeless college student, to getting married and leaving a mutually abusive relationship. I have had all the accolades and success at work, made history with my accomplishments and shared as much as I could along the way. I married the love of my life and have a beautiful daughter, who is a healthy and happy human. I have suffered tremendous loss and learned that sometimes I need help, I can't do things all on my own.

Although I have so much more to learn and do, I am living the best version of myself thus far and I love who I am and who I am becoming. I acknowledge I could not be here had it not been for the characters in my life who taught me tough lessons, and for that I am thankful.

Serving others is one of the most rewarding acts that you can perform. Service truly comes from the heart and requires humility. Whatever you do, do it with a heart of service and the gifts you will receive in turn are priceless.

Build and foster meaning relationships along your journey. Both personally and professionally, we need a circle that will stretch us for growth and push us to the next level to achieve our destiny. Be deliberate about your relationships and value the time you have with the people who mean something to you. Recently I lost someone who was near and dear to my heart, my "Butterfly." It was so sudden and so unexpected, and I'm still just not over it. I think of her every day, and it has caused a shift in my thinking concerning who I spend my time with, what relationships I value, and just simply how precious time is. I'm sure it is something that we have all experienced in some way or another, but I have become very deliberate about spending time with the people who I care about and who care about me. Relationships are so important; stop taking them for granted. Stop telling people, "Let's do coffee," or "Let's do lunch," and never do it. When someone is on your mind, reach out, because one day it will be too late!

I have come a LONG way from being that homeless girl staring at the ceiling in a dark living room with nowhere to go. I have endured struggles and made many sacrifices; I have been triumphant and blessed; I have been mistreated, yet protected when I didn't know I needed protection. Through it all, I have gained lifelong relationships along the way. In the darkest days, I encourage you to always remember to never give up! It will not be easy, but I promise it will be worth it. You have earned your seat at the table; we have a responsibility to take our seat and prepare a place for those coming after us, continuing the legacy of being 'Unstoppable!'

ABOUT DR. ALISHA SMITH

Dr. Alisha Smith is the owner and founder of L.I.N.C. Consulting, LLC. She was born and raised in San Jose, California, and is a retired Veteran after humbling serving twenty-eight years in the US Air Force as a Hospital Administrator. Her diverse career incorporates leadership at all levels. She has led built and led multi-functional teams, values mentorship and thrives on building relationships.

Dr. Smith is an avid learner who holds a doctorate degree in Health Sciences with a focus on Global Health Studies from A.T. Still University and three master's degrees; however, her greatest accomplishments are being the wife of Bruce and mother of Kiana.

LinkedIn: www.linkedin.com/in/dr-alisha-smith-1b872063

14

CINDY MORTON-FERREIRA

THE CINDERELLA EFFECT – WORK TREND

here does the fairytale start and end. In a world that there is so much access to information and data, how do you know where to start and what is real. In the pursuit of been unstoppable, there was a clear driver for me to ensure that I was successful, but with that came the fear of what if I am not able to measure up and be able to meet people where they need and ultimately want me. What if I share and people use that against me, and I guarantee there will be people that use your vulnerability and see it to conquer you and your position but please hold fast to your courage and always remember that your vulnerability is wherein your finest strength lies.

THE MOMENT OF TRUTH

Let's start this Fairy tale off like many others... once upon a time there was a fair maiden that did average at school, worked hard but did not get the highest results and her passion and drive was in a craft that allowed for her creative potential to share her true thinking and wanting to create an environment for children to dance. But she had a glimpse in her eye that allowed her to venture into her first business at a tender age of 8. And that glimpse was unknown but during her exposure to the world... the glimpse was named HOPE.

The fairytale was followed up with reality and that the passion to create an environment for children to dance could be replaced with a passion for the empowerment of people and creation of new businesses.

Let's continue in faith and discuss where the levers lie that would be the unlock that has had dramatic results and massively accelerated change in the world of the princess and the knight coming to her rescue. Is that still prevalent in our current environments and how do we manage to manoeuvre past this key perception of how a woman must show up and what it will take to make women unstoppable to reach that pinnacle? The princess is now her own saviour and does not have to have a knight rescue the situation.

I advocate for my amazing career and all the remarkable opportunities I have obtained and that my journey albeit challenging has always been worth so much in terms of lessons learned and growing. I have come into various corporations and have had to meet my clients where they are at but have always entrusted that inner voice (called intuition) and ensured that I live my truth and own my voice and yes sometimes the voice might have a quiver, but it will always be a factual, logical delivery that is sometimes challenging the situations and having the hard conversations.

I am getting ahead of myself and my fairytale. It is not much of a leap for me to start off as my Cinderella Effect and how it made me relook the glass slipper and know that I was going to do whatever it took for me to achieve special moments. I had obtained years of experience, training and of course observation in the corporate world and entrepreneurial business adventures but with all of that I was convinced that I needed to make clear path in honing one master skill of been fearless. There is always that inner voice and sometimes it is not so inner... that warns you, to take a leap of faith, and to encourage moments that you will have to consistently have the power to be courageous and know that it is ok to fail. A month into me starting on my own and having presented and achieved my first corporate client, my health tripped me up and the pause button was quickly hit as I had to chase the survival journey. I had been diagnosed with a brain tumour that was aggressive and needed to be removed. After a successful operation and an accelerated period of healing, I had to look myself in the mirror and say dust yourself off and start by firstly getting myself back into the working environment. There were key changes to my world ~one key item was my manner in which I spoke and I had to learn new skills to ensure that this was not going to hold me back in a world of speaking. My career driven by using my voice to impart the story and the learnings and then help motivate people to look within themselves and to know that it is ok to be imperfect and that more than anything you need to have compassion for yourself and others which leads you to be authentic in who you are and how you show up.

Women often find themselves shouldering additional responsibilities and facing disproportionate challenges compared to their counterparts and normally not only at the hand of men and themselves but more often than not at the hand of the "Evil Stepmother" that has also faced the societal norms and instead of promoting gender diversity has looked at accommodating the behaviour and perpetuating the male traits to succeed in business. We all have that niggling voice that guides us to do things and as I embarked on my career with the bump in the road and again faced the Cinderella effect that I was in the cinders needing to work my way through the ashes to get to the top.

LEANING INTO YOUR TRUTH

I did not grow up where a lot of women went to university and got degrees instead, I was faced with many that had been dedicated in terms of looking after their families, which sometimes meant just getting jobs that they worked hard at and put food on the table.

Earning an income is a source of earning respect and been able to ensure that you are looking after your family should be a true reflection of our power and that most decisions in life are based on love and responsibility for women. I had made conscious decisions around my career and my education and started my career swiftly and then studied part time, which meant I did study for many, many years. But that was the truth of what I had wanted to do was participate in a world of the ARTS and continue to grow my knowledge base so that I would have the opportunity to start a business or a corporate career when the time was right.

How do we keep women growing in our workforce if we do not lean into the truth of reassessment and valuing women on their own terms and the amazing positive energies that they are able to impart in a business context even when ensuring they are being the best part of themselves.

To break the Cinderella effect, as a fearless women leader, I have had to consciously embark on the journey of self-observation and start believing in what I am able to achieve. There are some simple key ideas that us as a community need to share with our societies that will continue to develop and shape the future of our fearless leaders. In general, men attribute their successes to themselves and what they have achieved but as a norm, women attribute their successes to others and other factors that influenced them into that role.

There are some key items that I would like to explore with the future leaders and with my associates around how to ensure that this topic does not continue to drag through to the next generation but that we also address some of these challenges and ensure we are able to implement with equality for all, not just a drive to push women into positions but also educate and enlighten the generation of men to what women can truly add to business, families and ultimately society in their various communities.

Firstly, remember that you are not alone in facing these challenges or versions of these challenges and there are more networks available to help you overcome them. That we can all create a more balanced and fulfilling career path that will allow you to aspire to your values and ensure that you speak your truth and start ensuring that your energies are aligned.

Here are some strategies that you can implement and drive to break the Cinderella Effect and ensure that the cinders no longer linger on your path.

- Lead by Example - serve as a role model for other women by demonstrating resilience, professionalism and determination in the face of adversity. Be a storyteller of your experiences and insights to inspire and empower others to navigate similar challenges.
- Set Realistic Expectations - Understand that you cannot do everything perfectly all the time. Set realistic expectations for yourself in each of your roles; from the career to your family and prioritise tasks based on their importance and impact it will have overall.
- Learn to communicate your boundaries - Clearly learn to set and communicate your boundaries. Do not be afraid to say no to additional tasks or ask for support.
- Challenge perceptions - Do not internalise societal norms about how women should balance their roles as mothers, daughters, wives and professionals. Challenge the stereotypes by demonstrating that you can excel or ensure you get assistance without having to sacrifice one for the other or your health.
- Set up support networks - Surround yourself with supportive mentors, colleagues, friends and family that are able to understand the challenges you face. Most importantly, learn to lean on these networks for encouragement and advice and sometimes just a break.
- Invest in Self Care - Prioritise self-care to maintain your physical and emotional well-being. Take time for yourself

to recharge and pursue activities outside of the work balance that bring you joy and fulfilment.

- Advocate for yourself - Make sure your contributions are recognised and valued. Discuss your opportunities for advancement and your career aspirations. It is important to find the correct balance between being assertive and being collaborative.

REFLECTION OF MY FEARLESS LEADERSHIP JOURNEY

So as the years have rolled into each other and my career has taken me in many boardrooms, platforms and in front of many people to mentor and guide, I can gracefully and passionately look back onto the herstory and say I fondly remember saying I do believe that I can do anything and I know that when I have a few grey hairs of knowledge it will address the inexperience of the dilemmas that I have faced in certain circumstances.

Not everyone of us is going to attain C-level leadership, but leadership is not about position but rather about the action we take that embraces all aspects of the authenticity and breaking the status quo by allowing your female insights to deliver to success in your world and creating a legacy that teaches current and future generations that the world needs female and males to be unstoppable and that we all add to this amazing boiling pot of business that allows us to be change fit and in those terms deliver to continued growth of business that will align to future fit yourself to the industries that will be developing and taking our communities into the next big thing.

It is truly inspiring to hear about the journey and reflection of the trailblazing women that have influenced my career. Throughout herstory, there have been countless remarkable women, from the moms and teachers in our communities to women that defied societal norms and expectations to lead with courage, vision and resilience. Many of these women faced significant challenges and obstacles, however their contributions have had a profound impact on shaping the world we live and work in today.

It is understandable to have high expectations for yourself, especially when your inspired by the extraordinary achievements of others. However, it is important to always remember and understand that not everyone's journey is the same and it is unique to you, and you are allowed to forgive yourself for not always meeting your standards that you have set.

Fearless female leaders are amongst us and continue to walk as mere mortals in our communities and families and it is of the utmost that as a culture, we should recognise the achievements of these leaders and honour their legacies to ensure that the power of the intent is an incredible lesson for all. They serve as role models for us and future generations, demonstrating the power of perseverance, determination and resilience in the face of adversity.

Remember that as a women albeit in a corporate world, a family space, teachers and mothers to the future generations, as you reflect on your own journey and the impact that the women around you have, it is my wish that you find your inspiration and strength in their stories to allow yourself to be the story teller that allows your legacy to shine and grow with each development. You are enough. You are powerful. You have all that you require within you to move and be part of the legacy we are sharing daily. Your own contributions are valuable and worthy of recognition. Keep embracing your unique path and never underestimate the impact that you can have on the world around you.

VALUING WOMEN ON THEIR OWN TERMS

In conclusion for us as a community and to address the people, men and women, on the key values that need to be tackled in our work environments and in our personal spaces, my thoughts are that we must ensure that key things are worth fighting for.

Valuing family as part of the role to ensure that people deliver to their voices and speak their truths, there are a couple of items that need to be put into place.

Firstly, get women to sit at the table and do not perpetuate the gender bias that they are either there to take notes or make the coffee. Women need to work on the belief that they can do anything that they put their minds to, and that the world will adjust to their requirements. If you make decisions based on love and responsibility, then you are making the decisions that will allow that 1% of change to happen in your environments.

This is not an initiative that only has to be addressed by women, but it must be addressed by society and ensure that the voice of all the people is heard and that we teach our generations that we can all be fearless leaders and become unstoppable.

ABOUT CINDY MORTON-FERREIRA

Cindy is a dynamic and influential figure in the world of corporate culture, change management, and leadership. With a successful career spanning both South Africa and international markets, she has garnered extensive experience and insights that she now shares as a best-selling author and speaker.

Her expertise lies in fostering enterprise change and cultivating organizational agility to thrive in an ever-evolving business landscape. Cindy's passion for walking the talk of leadership and instigating transformative growth sets her apart as an unstoppable force in her field.

Not content with just her own accomplishments, Cindy has embarked on a new venture to mentor and support aspiring authors. Through her diverse career journey and unwavering commitment to learning and development, Cindy embodies the ethos of continuous improvement and resilience. Her dedication to fostering positive change and amplifying voices underscores her status as a trailblazer in both the corporate and literary realms.

Websites: *www.cindymortonferreira.com*
www.dnaatworx.co.za
LinkedIn: *www.linkedin.com/in/cindymortonferreira*

15

HOLLY R. TAYLOR

LET YOUR "NOS" LEAD YOUR WAY

WOMEN WERE ALLOWED IN THE NAVY, BUT NOT ON ITS SHIPS

Some people think that resilience is something you're born with, and others think that it's something you develop as you face life's challenges. Who's to say how much resilience I was born with? But what I do know is this: I've been told "No" countless times in my fifty years. And whether you want to call it nature or nurture, I never once let the "Nos" hold me back from what I wanted out of life.

I grew up in a tiny town in Louisiana. Like—I graduated high school with only 18 people – tiny. In a town like that, it's easy to stand out. I stood out because I was good at basketball. I dreamed of playing for a big college. I wanted to stand out to recruiters and take my skills to the college courts. Convincing my father to give me this shot, however, proved to be difficult. He had reservations about my transitioning to a larger school environment, fearing that it might overwhelm me. My first "No."

I lost faith in my ability to be recognized by college recruiters, but I didn't let it stop my passion for the game. I lead my team to a State Championship. I won the Best Defensive Player award. I was recognized as an All State Academic. This was my first lesson in building resilience. I had dreams of going places as a basketball star. Ones that, as a teenager, I could never fulfill without the support of my family.

Unfortunately, this isn't the part where I tell you that despite the odds, I was able to secure a spot on a college team. I played my last basketball game ever during my senior year in high school. I had dreams of playing in college and going on to be a coach. None of that came true, because sometimes, life doesn't play out the way you want it to. But resilience is about picking up another dream when life tells you your old ones won't work out. Resilience is dreaming big regardless of your circumstances.

With my dreams of basketball in the rearview mirror, I started at a local college near my home. I was pursuing a nursing degree, even though it was not my passion. I always held great respect for nurses, but it was never what I saw for myself. Since my education was not something I could finance on my own, I felt compelled to adhere to the expectations set for me by my family, and so I remained in this major.

I had no real idea about the direction I wanted my life to take. But in the back of my head, always, I thought: "This isn't it." Call it delusion or blind optimism, but I knew I could be somebody in this world and pursue something I felt passionate about. I knew I was meant for more than what this tiny little town could offer me. So, I started planning.

A friend from high school had joined the military, and her parents shared with me how the GI Bill would cover her college education. This information sparked a lightbulb moment for me. Realizing that joining the Navy could offer me the same opportunity to have my college funded, I saw a way to pursue a career path of my own choosing, beyond the constraints of what was expected of me. I could go on to be something, anything, else away from this tiny town. I snuck off to the Navy recruiting office and signed the contract.

A lot of people join the military to escape their lives, but I joined the military so I could start mine. I wanted agency. I wanted to be a player in my life's game. I wanted to call the shots, even if it meant signing my life away for a few years. It would be worth it in the end if I could just build a life that was my own.

That's how I ended up in Alaska.

MY FIRST STOP IN THE NAVY: ALASKA

In the early 90's, women weren't allowed on combat ships, so I was stationed in Adak, Alaska, working in Logistics. This station was the first of many things for me. The first time I worked in a male-dominated space. The first time I'd heard personally disparaging comments, because of my gender. The first time I second-guessed my decision to leave home and join the Navy. And of course, the first of many "Nos" I'd hear throughout my time serving.

For a while, I let those voices fill my head. I kept remembering my goal was to get the GI Bill and get out. I didn't try much harder than that. I drank too much. I didn't care about my military bearing. I didn't even care my uniform was wrinkled every day. To advance in the Navy, I had to take an exam based on information I would have learned on a ship... if I had been allowed on one. It was unfair and that fueled my apathy. I didn't pass the first time. To be honest, I hadn't even studied.

The moment I started feeling the weight of my indifference was when my Chief told me that he'd never once had someone work for him that didn't pass the exam. This lit a fire in me. I was determined to not be his first failure.

After that, I started using the "Nos," the disparaging comments, and the inequities I faced, as fuel. I knew what I was faced with was unfair, but I never let that keep me from playing the game again. I became disciplined in my studies. I was determined to advance, despite my lack of hands-on experience on a ship. And to the surprise of many people who expected my failure was imminent, I passed the exam.

Sometimes, life does tell you "No," and there isn't anything you can do about it. Sometimes though, those setbacks are all on you. The negative situations you put yourself in often teach you more about the kind of person you want to be.

While I was in logistics, I witnessed a friend commit a small crime. I did nothing about it. When we got caught, I was punished for not speaking up and ultimately, for not acting with integrity. For thirty days, I was escorted everywhere I went. I wore a special uniform that acted as a Scarlet A. I was humiliated. Honestly. It's not a memory I choose to relive often.

But it was a major step for me in building my resilience. When you start to realize that your choices, good and bad, will ultimately turn you into the person you want to be, you start acting with integrity. You start valuing reliability and trustworthiness. And you start promising yourself that you'll never again act in a way that will hold you back from what you want in life. And, to this day, I've done my best to keep that promise.

THE ONE PERSON WHO NEVER TOLD ME NO

Before I move on, I need to tell you about the one person in my life who has always told me "Yes." My jaw dropped when I first saw Jerry. He was powerful and attractive. He was quite literally out of my league, because of our difference in rank. However, as I've alluded to, I am relentless and wouldn't let that stop me. I sent him flowers every week for three weeks. Every time they arrived, he got more and more irate about his secret admirer.

Jerry eventually found out that it was me. To say, "and the rest is history," wouldn't be an accurate depiction of our lives together. We've had many ups and downs. We got married without telling a soul in the Navy. We've moved all over the world together. We've lived separately for years because of our deployments. He gave up his entire Navy career for me. We've had to navigate the transition into civilian life both separately and as a couple. But Jerry has never wavered in his belief in my abilities. He redefined for me what it meant to be supported and loved by someone. For that, I am forever grateful.

ACTUALLY, I THINK I'LL STICK AROUND

My initial goal of staying with the Navy only for the purpose of qualifying for the GI Bill was long gone. Once I had a taste of success, I wanted more. I started setting lofty goals for myself. Eventually, I started to believe that I could attain them. In 2001, seeking a career shift from Logistics to Legal, I requested my first assignment as a Legalman to be on independent duty with a Seabee Battalion. This would allow me to be closer to Jerry. As this is the theme of this chapter, you could probably guess that I was told "No." I was too junior. I wouldn't be able to handle it, they said, yet again.

Before my transfer to a ship out of Jacksonville, FL, I was called and asked if the Seabee Battalion was still where I wanted to be. No one else wanted to go there, and I was being given a shot. Life has a funny way of yanking you around until you end up right where you're supposed to be, and this station proved to be no different.

I was deployed to Puerto Rico once and Southwest Asia twice, including the initial invasion supporting Operations Enduring Freedom and Iraqi Freedom. I was the only Legalman there both times I went. Eventually, I was nominated for Legalman of the Year for the entire U.S. Navy.

If you know anything about me, you know that what I value the most in the world is support and community. That is largely in part to the impact my mentor, Jimmy, had on my life.

I met Jimmy when I was stationed with the Seabees. He was one of the first superiors I ever had who treated me like I was special, like

I mattered. He believed that I could be somebody. He wanted to see me succeed, but that never meant taking it easy on me. Quite the opposite. He made me tough. I can still hear him yelling, "Suck it up, Seabee!" to me when I wanted to give up.

Years later, I was waiting to hear whether I'd made Chief Petty Officer (E7) when I became eligible. I'd been told I'd never advance to that level because I had never spent time on a ship. A call came in on my cell, and I looked down to see that it was my mentor calling. I immediately knew I'd done it, and that he'd be the one to give me the news. Every time I've doubted myself since, I remember his unwavering belief in me. And because of him, I've always valued offering support to someone else who could possibly change the trajectory of their lives.

MENTORING OTHERS BECAUSE I WAS MENTORED FIRST

Thanks to my mentor, I made it my mission many times to push those who couldn't see their capabilities. If you lacked belief in yourself, I was your girl. I would wake up at 5:00 AM to run miles with you. I'd meet you in the gym to spot you through your reps. I'd get in your face and yell at you until you finally believed what you were capable of. If I hadn't had my mentor, I don't know where I'd be today. I was determined to be that person for as many as I possibly could. And I watched a lot of them soar. If I wasn't going to let "No" deter me, I wasn't going to let it deter you, either.

As I was advancing in my career, and mentoring others, I realized I wanted to become an officer. I decided to apply for the JAG Corps Limited Duty Officer program because I wanted to continue to work in the Legal community. The year that I became eligible to apply, the program was disestablished. This left me with two options – go the Administrative route or the Security route. Admin was typically reserved for Yeomen and Personnelmen, and Security was typically reserved for Masters-at-Arms. I was none of those. Because I'd earned my warfare designation and had experience in military law and weapons, I decided to try my hand at Security.

I was told I'd never be accepted for this program because of my lack of experience. I was told that if I was, I'd never be accepted within the Security ranks. They were right about only one of those statements. I was accepted into Security on my first application, but I never felt like I belonged there.

FINDING OUT WHAT BELONGING MEANS

On my first night at my new duty station as a Security Officer, my roommate told me that that they didn't like, "people like me coming into their community without Masters-at-Arms experience." A very warm greeting. For my first tour in security, I was sent to Guantanamo Bay to guard enemy combatants. I wasn't welcomed there either. My time there taught me this about resilience: you can believe what they say about you, or you can believe what YOU say about you.

For me, mindset was everything. Though I was constantly told I didn't belong and wouldn't be good at my job, I had long since learned to ignore those voices. I had built up mental resilience at this point which allowed me to brush off the naysayers with confidence. I thrived on proving people wrong. I didn't need to belong to be successful.

Did I miss having community and support? Of course. But instead of looking around for others to accept me, I focused on building my own community and support system wherever I could. This skill has proved valuable to me at every turn – especially in retirement.

I was moved to the Strategic Weapons Facility as the First Female Naval Officer with Marine Corps Security Force Battalion, Kings Bay, GA. The station was split: half Navy, half Marine Corps. The warm greetings continued.

There was a Marine Captain that always seemed to have a problem with me. I couldn't break through to him –I was over it. I asked him what his problem was with me, to which he replied, "Women belong in Logistics or Admin." I guess, at least, I could take solace in the fact that it wasn't personal to me, just my gender.

At this point, I had been considering a change to Admin because I knew it would be good for my career. To be honest, I didn't want to prove all those men right – that women, including me, belonged in Admin. It was a struggle for me to finally accept that it was the best move for my career, despite the stigma attached. The truth is, while I had done well in different departments I'd been in, Admin was most aligned with my skillset. I was and am organized to fault, detail-oriented, and meticulous.

I always felt like I should ignore those parts of me so that I could be seen as tough. I didn't want to be an "Office Bitch" or stuck behind a desk. I'd built my reputation as someone who was always down for action, who could handle every situation, who never complained about the rough living quarters, and who would run to the trouble, not away from it. Detail-oriented and meticulous were skills not needed in security.

Turns out, knowing what your strengths are and using them to do a damn good job, can be pretty badass too. I was the Executive Officer and Admin Officer for the Navy's Blue Angels. I served as the Ship Secretary and Personnel Officer for the U.S.S. Carl Vinson, where I also earned my Surface Warfare Pin and qualified to drive the ship. I ended my career as one of three female department heads onboard the U.S.S Eisenhower, which was the first Aircraft carrier in the Navy that allowed women to serve.

But of course, I heard my share of "Nos" in these positions, too.

I CHOSE FEAR OVER INTEGRITY

At one point, I struggled for the first time in my life with fear. Fear of speaking up and facing retaliation, fear of being a "tattle-tail," fear of making it even more clear to everyone around me that I was not "one of the guys."

Pornography taped to the walls was the norm. Slurs about sexual orientation were encouraged. Sexually explicit humor was the norm. To be honest, *this is the PG version.*

I watched it all happen. I never participated. But I was complicit. I never stopped it. I watched another female speak up about it. She was berated. I'd worked so hard to get where I was, that I thought surely, I could just deal with it for a while longer.

What I never expected was this: years and years later, I'm still dealing with my choice to remain silent. I feel guilty about this period of my life. I knew what the right thing to do was and I did nothing because I was afraid.

Most people would look at this situation and think, "Holly, why should you have been the sacrificial lamb?" I get it. I agree to some point. But I'd made a promise to myself to act with integrity. To me, staying silent when I should've spoken up wasn't integrous. It was weak. I operated with fear as the driving force in my life during this time in my career.

It's easy for me to look back on that period of my life with shame. But life is about taking the good with the bad, isn't it? While I'm not proud of myself for my inaction, I can see how it shaped the person I am now. Simply put, I am not the person anymore who stays silent in the face of injustice. Also, I've learned to give myself grace. Often, we're just doing the best we can do, at the time, in the circumstances we find ourselves. Resilience isn't just built in hard-fought battles, it's also won when you accept your limitations, forgive yourself for them, and continue to do better.

MY UNEXPECTED RETIREMENT

Most people in the military have a general plan for when they'll retire: after a certain number of years, once they reach a certain rank, etc. I never did. I'd been in for 26 years, and genuinely saw no end in sight for myself. I'd had success and wanted more of it. The Navy had turned out to be so much more than just a 4-year path to the GI Bill.

It had taken me all over the world and across a couple of oceans. I'd done and seen more than I ever could've imagined at 18 as my basketball dreams vanished.

Under the typical sea/shore rotation, it's customary to serve two years of sea duty followed by a rotation on shore duty for two years. After transitioning from one ship, I had only six months of shore duty before being asked and agreeing to return to sea duty. I had been on ships for the last 4 years – the U.S.S. Carl Vinson and then the U.S.S. Eisenhower. After 4 years on sea duty, my only options were unaccompanied tours overseas without my husband. This was the last "No" I'd hear in the Navy. This was a line in the sand that I would not cross. I had done my duty. I decided I wouldn't be taken advantage of anymore. So, I retired.

The next chapter of my life began.

To say I was unprepared for this phase of my life is an enormous understatement. I'd never considered what I'd do in retirement because I'd never considered retiring. I'd never grown a professional network because I never thought I'd need one. I never even had a resumé because I'd never applied for a civilian job. Basically, I had no idea where to start.

I applied for a PhD program and finished two semesters before my GI Bill ran out. I folded yoga pants at Lululemon for a while. I worked the opening shift at a cookie shop, baking hundreds of cookies before they opened at 8:00 AM. I was partially lost, and partially OK with not having it all figured out. I thought I'd try the corporate world when I didn't find the PhD program fulfilling, so I landed a job with one of the biggest online e-commerce platforms in the world that "sounds like a jungle" and frankly, for many employees, it really can be (I am not revealing its name intentionally as part of my ethical code and to share my story fully). I had dealt with so much adversity throughout my 26 years in the Navy. To be honest, I never thought that Corporate America could ever throw anything at me that I couldn't handle. I was built tough after all I'd faced. I thought that the resilience I built up meant I could face anything.

While I had faced a lot of challenges professionally in the Navy, I had never had them coupled with personal challenges as well. During my time at this organization, I faced both. The environment that I worked in was extremely toxic, and, frankly, my boss was a bully. I thought as someone who had served her country for over two decades, the respect I'd earned would translate to this new workplace. It didn't work like that.

I remember being at my mother-in-law's funeral and receiving calls from my boss about work deadlines. The biggest shock came when I was diagnosed with breast cancer, and my appointments were treated like an inconvenience.

After even more losses gripped our family, I reached my breaking point. I was done trying to hold it all together. Again, I was reminded that resilience doesn't always mean carrying on when times get tough. It can sometimes mean accepting your limit, packing up, and doing what's best for you and your family. Sometimes all that resilience you've built up over the years serves this purpose: to teach you what you are and aren't willing to accept in your life.

I quit my job.

BUILDING THE LIFE YOU WANT TAKES HARD WORK

Once again, this isn't the part where I figured it all out. I was reeling from all that I'd been through and didn't know if I could handle another corporate working environment. I remembered some of the key lessons I'd learned in the Navy and started relentlessly pursuing them in my spare time. I started growing my professional network.

I continued my learning and education in a multitude of ways. I fostered relationships with the connections I'd made. I started telling my stories on social media, to whoever would listen. For a while, I got a job as a leadership coach with a consulting firm. I was told to wait around for an assignment that never came. I moved on.

Ultimately, I took this time to figure out what I wanted for my life. I refused to believe that the good parts of my life were past. I knew that with all the experience I'd gained and all the resilience I'd built, I could forge the rest of my life into whatever I wanted it to be. Fear of the unknown, fear of what others thought, fear of being told "No": none of those things scared me anymore. The only thing that kept me up at night was the possibility of not filling my days with purposeful work.

EVERY "NO" LED ME TO EXACTLY WHERE I WAS SUPPOSED TO BE

Initially, I started my business to support executives and entrepreneurs as a virtual assistant – and through this, I found meaningful work. I've been able to work with people who value my expertise. I've been able to showcase my stories and experience to thousands of people online. I navigated my transition out of the military with as much grace as I possibly could – which often, didn't feel like much. I landed on my feet. Now I get to help others do the same.

A girl with a dream of playing basketball. 26 years in the Navy. 3 years in Corporate America. 1 year as a business owner. Dozens of countries. Countless duty stations and ranks. Hundreds of "Nos" along the way. I never gave up.

I surrounded myself with good people who believed in me. I believed in myself when there was no one. Maybe I was born with resilience. Maybe I built it up over the last 50 years. Either way, whatever "No" life has in store for me next, I'm ready for it.

I welcome the challenge because I know that every "No" is both a lesson and a learning opportunity. I'm grateful for every single "No" I've already faced.

"Nos" led me right to where I am today.

Your "Nos" will, too.

ABOUT HOLLY R. TAYLOR

Holly Taylor, a trailblazer from a small town in Louisiana, chose an unconventional path, leaving college to enlist in the Navy for a journey that spanned 26 impactful years. With two deployments to Iraq and diverse roles, including Officer-in-Charge in Guantanamo Bay and Executive Officer for the Blue Angels, Holly's tenacity propelled her through the ranks. Simultaneously pursuing academic goals, she earned both bachelor's and master's degrees from the University of Alabama while serving actively.

Transitioning to Corporate America, she managed global crises across 21 countries, demonstrating unparalleled crisis management skills. Now an entrepreneur and leadership coach, Holly's narrative weaves resilience, adaptability, and optimism, showcasing her unique blend of military precision and corporate efficiency. Her journey from groundbreaking naval service to inspiring leadership in the corporate and entrepreneurial realms embodies the spirit of transformation and relentless optimism, making her an exemplary figure for aspiring leaders worldwide.

Website: *www.linkedin.com/in/hollybrasheartaylor*

16

DR. KACEE JONES

"BREATHE, IT'S JUST A CHAPTER, NOT YOUR WHOLE BOOK"

MY EARLY YEARS FRAMED MY VIEW OF *LOVE*

I was born as the third child of five in Topeka, Kansas, to parents who were married young, 17 and 18 respectively. There were five of us, four girls and our baby brother. They provided a roof and food, so I guess that would be considered *stable*. Until the age of seven, we lived in low-income projects in the north side of town. Our family was on food stamps and WIC—not so much because my dad didn't make money; it was his partying that absorbed it. Think partying of the 80s and you nailed it. If anyone had told me twenty years ago that I would be where I am today, I would have laughed at them.

Our mom was emotionally and psychologically abusive towards us. Her spite toward our father during their twenty-two-year marriage was redirected toward us. She yelled. She cursed. She called us terrible names. From my memory bank I can count five times hearing her say *I love you* to me. The same behavior from her carried into our adulthood. I have not spoken with her in years. As an adult, I had to guard my mental and emotional peace. We didn't receive hugs or bedtime stories, from either parent. I didn't understand as a child.

When you grow up not feeling love, you hope there is a solid extended family that can give it. Unfortunately, we grew up with very little ties to her side of the family. I say that because I probably couldn't name each of her siblings and have no clue how many children they had. I want to say she tried to integrate us with them a bit early on, but their blatant and passive racism really played a part in our nuclear family not being involved with that side. The things I do know of that side of the family come from my older sister. Sadly, she was old enough to remember some of the things that went on, both good and bad. It was through her memories I was able to piece together the enormous trauma my mom must have suffered growing up, too. Her mom was abusive. Her dad racist. She was molested by a sibling. Although, I am thankful she used that trauma in being over-protective with letting us kids be around certain people. Many of those people later were found to be pedophiles. Our dad also likely triggered her traumas. He cheated a lot. My oldest sister recalled when we were young our mom had to return our Easter outfits because he had blown all the bill money on partying. She told us the bags were accidentally thrown away to cover for him. Another time he was so out of it from partying that they got into a big fight, and he became aggressive, so she packed us kids up in the station wagon, gave us popsicles, and sat in the grocery store parking lot that faced our apartment until the lights went out, meaning he'd gone to sleep or left. The trickle effect of her childhood trauma and early adult-hood led her to unleash it on us as kids.

As for my dad, he wasn't always consistent in our lives even though my parents were married until I was 17. He was fighting his own battles that I didn't understand until I was much older. We had some sense of connection with his family, but we moved to a small town in the country when I was about seven. The distance between the town and Topeka was about an hour and a half. It was because of this we didn't often make it back to Topeka to spend time with his side of the family. Nonetheless, when it comes to family, that was the closest we had. I'm fairly certain our move to the country was also motivated by the need to get him out of the environment that exacerbated his partying. When he was present, I had fond memories of him cooking breakfast, coming to sports games, taking us fishing at a local pond, and waking us up at 4 a.m. to chop wood for the stove that heated our old farmhouse.

I'd like to think that my parents weren't purposefully inactive in showing us love or guidance. I truly believe they came from the generations that swept trauma under the rug, and no one wanted to talk about it. I think their trauma spilled over to us, yet they still never really understood. I remember discovering through an at-home DNA test that my dad's father could not have been his biological father. When word got out, I was told by a family member that we don't speak about those things and leave it alone. His mother, my grandmother, passed away when I was 2. This meant we grew up with no grandparents and virtually no close-knit family. My dad does acknowledge now how his struggles negatively impacted us. Somedays I fear it is too late to truly mend and build a strong bond with him. I do thank him for my love of 80s rock and cravings for his family's enchilada recipe.

GROWING UP IN THE COUNTRY TAUGHT ME MANY SKILLS, BUT LITTLE ABOUT SOCIAL CONNECTIONS

Spending most of my formative years in the country, I learned a lot of skills that I am thankful for to this day, but I still didn't learn much about love and meaningful connections. I was able to enjoy nature, the freedom of outdoors with no real limits, and the education was far superior to Topeka. However, the seclusion of growing up in a town of less than 200 people and not having the guidance of a close parental relationship contributed to me developing socially behind other kids my age—though, I am extremely thankful for my oldest sister and our relationship. She consistently kept the glue hanging on when we were isolated living there from trips to the country mart with coin change to buy bread or making shepherd's pie before we knew it was a real thing. We still call each other and share stories and memories that we both tucked so far back in our memory bank. I could never blame her for moving away when she turned 18. I mean our dad bought her luggage for her birthday. Each of us siblings developed differently from these experiences.

HIGH SCHOOL MARKED A PIVOTAL MOMENT IN MY LIFE WHERE I HAD TO START DEFINING WHAT LOVE MEANT AND DIDN'T MEAN

The beginning of high school in 1996 marked a significant chapter for our family as we relocated back to Topeka. Little did I anticipate the profound culture shock that awaited me, not only in terms of the academic environment but also within the realm of social dynamics. The transition from a relatively sheltered existence to what I could only describe as the "real world" left me feeling astounded and somewhat overwhelmed. I was unsure of how to seamlessly integrate into this new, unfamiliar life.

No one wants to think of themselves as a textbook case of looking for love or acceptance in all the wrong places because you didn't get it growing up. That was me, though. The first person to tell me they *loved me* when I had nothing to compare it to, had me, because I believed it. I was so naive. Unfortunately, when you meet the wrong people and you don't know what respect and love is supposed to feel like, you think what they give you is what you deserve. It didn't help when the first individual that I connected with after moving back from the country was somebody who had negative intentions. It was too easy to latch on because I was desperate to feel love.

The first person who told me they loved me I immediately attached to. Now that I am older, I know he targeted girls that didn't have much self-worth because we were easier to control. He was just a few years older than me. Not surprisingly, I ended up pregnant by him in 1998 at 16 and a sophomore in high school—he was 19. I was scared. Having parents that didn't pay much attention to me, I was able to hide it until I was nearly seven months along. My parents offered no support. I remember my mom's exact words when I told them, she said "oh well that's on you." My dad just expressed his regret for moving us back to Topeka. They were going through toxic relationship issues which had languished most of their marriage and ultimately led to their divorce a few years later. I was sent to the *bad kids'* school as I called it. It was the only high school in the area at the time with a daycare. Going to a non-traditional high school only furthered my isolation and kept me from building social bonds or even enjoying my teen years. I didn't go to games. I didn't go to prom. I didn't experience high school events. I struggled through working, going to classes during the day, and night school, while taking care of my daughter. I graduated a semester early and was renting a storage closet as a room from a friend that worked at the mall with me, who knew I needed a place to stay.

Nothing could have prepared me for teenage parenthood, especially with the added challenge of my daughter's father being inconsistent in her upbringing. His short visits with her always coincidently coincided with my paydays. He was unreliable with showing up for her, and it began to negatively impact her. Financial struggles compounded my difficulties, as neither he nor either of our families provided any support. The dynamics from his family were always centered around what I could do for them, without them having reciprocal consideration for me as a single mother. The situation worsened with his manipulative and toxic family, eroding my confidence and ability to set boundaries. They knew he was not providing for her. There was a lot of intimidation. My daughter was stuck with no grandparents or reliable relatives.

THE TURNING POINT CAME WHEN I CUT TIES WITH HIS FAMILY

The turning point came when my daughter was about five—I decisively cut ties with him and his family. I later learned it spared my daughter from the mistreatment she had experienced during contact with them. Her newfound comfort in discussing the trauma affirmed the wisdom of my choice to continue life as a single parent. Despite the challenges, I maintained resilience, keeping my head barely above water. The lack of efforts from his family to maintain contact or build a bond with my daughter after my decision only validated the need for this separation, allowing me and my daughter to navigate life just the two of us.

THE MULTI-LAYERED TRAUMA HIT ME HEAD-ON

I can now recognize how trauma contributed to me struggling with low self-worth. I felt constant criticism and emotional neglect during childhood that led to feelings of inadequacy as I became a young adult. I did not receive the emotional support I needed as a child, which led to a diminished sense of self-worth. Ultimately, this continued me on a path of difficulty in forming healthy relationships. My low self-esteem contributed to my fear of rejection or abandonment, which made it hard for me to assert healthy boundaries. I struggled to prioritize my own needs and was more susceptible to accepting mistreatment. While it may not always have been a good thing, I became laser focused on accomplishing more. I developed perfectionistic tendencies. I believed that by achieving high standards, I could finally gain a sense of self-worth. Rock bottom and what it cost me was coming; I just didn't know it yet.

Unfortunately, when you do not address or even understand the impact of how trauma plays out in your life, it makes you susceptible to repeated damages. This continued to lead me to being naive in other situations. The real rock bottom was when I ended up pregnant at the age of 19 by someone significantly older and with ill intentions. My lack of discernment led again to manipulation and unrest.

I felt lost, suicidal, and completely worthless as I was trapped in a system by the state that made it nearly impossible for a poor marginalized girl like me to seek an abortion. There were so many hoops to jump. The state created those barriers on purpose. I think about the fact I was sleeping on the floor during this time and making less than $8 per hour and didn't even have a car. In my apartment was a black and white TV, VHS tapes, and a toddler bed. I was still trying to navigate the role of being the only provider for my daughter let alone being forced to carry something in me for which I hated myself. A handful of people knew this, yet no one stepped up to offer me support. The negative emotional and mental impact was extreme and irreparable for many years. I tried to run from my problems for a short while, but it all led me back to Topeka to deal with it.

I HIT ROCK BOTTOM AND KNEW SOMETHING NEEDED TO CHANGE

After that trauma, I knew something in my life needed to change. An evaluation of my life was a clear indication that the choices I had made were not good. I was at rock bottom. It cost me my dignity and self-worth. I was determined to not let my daughter experience the same trauma I did and to give her better. Finally, I looked to where my heart had always found acceptance and passion: education and learning. I enrolled in our local university and began my undergraduate studies. Little did I know how that one decision would lead to so many exciting adventures in my life.

It was 2004 when I enrolled in college and when I met my first set of friends. It is insane to think I went all my formative years and teens without any type of social connection to a group of friends. However, once I met a group of girls in the university cafeteria, they absolutely lit my life up. I understood what it felt to be a part of a social circle and feel alive. Immediately these ladies took me under their wing and allowed me to be authentically me. I thrived with them by my side. They applauded me and corrected me along the way.

College was a whirlwind of fun and the budding of forever friendships. We enjoyed making so many memories and encouraging one another as we all grew from young adulthood to mature women. Me and my daughter moved into a small, old, but homely house. I bought my first car. I had frequent Sunday dinners at my place and trips with the girls to the only R&B club in the area. It wasn't until I met these ladies that I understood I was an individual who was worthy of love and acceptance no matter what. While working and through school, I also met two more people who also became life-long best friends. Those friends have continuously shown me grace and that family does not have to mean *blood*.

IN COLLEGE I WAS ABLE TO UNDERSTAND, DEFINE, AND FEEL LOVE

I don't want to say everything prior to 22 was a regret, but I have resolved that my decisions were not healthy or indicative of the woman I wanted to be. I was starved for acceptance and my traumas played a role in how my decisions shaped my life and brought me down. Having friends helped as I was able to confide in them and they always encouraged me to live freely. Although, I found myself still struggling in the first year of college and understanding why I had never connected in intimate relationships with anyone. The detachment I felt with any man in an intimate setting seemed to linger no matter who it was.

Everything I learned in life until that point taught me to live a certain way and within the societal norm. It wasn't until I met who became my first girlfriend that I realized how intimacy and attraction was supposed to feel. It finally all started to make sense when I went with friends to the college's regional women's basketball tournament. It was then that I saw her for the first time.

I felt a physical and emotional shock I had never felt before. I am not one to say love at first sight is real, but it felt like it. I was drawn to her physical appearance. I must acknowledge that while instant attraction can be a thrilling experience, building a healthy and lasting relationship requires time, communication, and mutual understanding—more on that later. The initial attraction was surface level, but as I got to know her on a deeper level, my feelings evolved in more meaningful ways. It was my first real relationship. My first love.

There was immediate and palpable chemistry between us that eventually led to a strong physical and emotional connection. It was the first time in my life that I felt so many exciting feelings at once. There was an energy we had and deep attraction that defied any bump in the road we experienced. I would spend days in her dorm room, so much so people thought I went to school there. I bonded with her roommates and became life-long friends with them. She and I shared a few years together, but it was frequently plagued by her insatiable need for attention resulting in numerous cheating instances and subsequent heartbreaks for me. I had never loved that deeply, so it hurt.

Ultimately, the fun of college ended, and she went back home to Phoenix, and although we tried for a little bit, we went our separate ways for a few years. She and I kept in contact over the years. I did some dating here and there but avoided starting a solid relationship, both intentional and not so intentional. I was tired of any drama attached to dating.

I RECLAIMED MY SELF-WORTH AND CONFIDENCE AND BEGAN MY PROFESSIONAL CAREER

I graduated college and in late 2007 I was able to secure my first professional job with the state as a case manager. I had a budding brief relationship that fizzled shortly after starting. But, after only one year at the state working, I was promoted to manager over the region. There was a sense of my first tangible career accomplishment. I was starting my ascent into feeling accomplished. I was good at my job. I was able to support myself and my kid. However, I had developed an insistent desire to dissociate myself from my upbringing and the state in which I was raised. After I left it took me more than a decade to even return for a visit. I was determined to shine.

It was in 2009, recognizing the limitations of opportunities in Kansas, I made the bold decision to enroll in my first master's program and relocate to Texas. This move was driven by my desire for a career that aligned with my education and aspirations. Despite facing a substantial pay cut, I embarked on this journey to the DFW area, where things initially took time to blossom. I remained persistent.

I spent several years of my career at a county hospital, and it was there that I encountered what I consider my first major professional breakthrough. Climbing the ranks, I earned the position of Policy Coordinator for the district, a role that not only bolstered my career but also ignited a passion within me. I hated my boss, but the experience paved the way for an opportunity at another health system, providing me with the chance to enhance my skills further. This set the stage for me finding my niche in my professional life. I was good at it.

During my five productive years in Texas, I cultivated numerous positive experiences, from an enriching connection with an amazing church community to fostering meaningful relationships with my partner's parents. My daughter also thrived in this new social environment, excelling in various aspects of her life. However, reflecting on my romantic relationship at the time, I now recognize a lack of compatibility that became increasingly apparent. Haunted by the trauma of infidelity from my first partner, I hyper-focused on loyalty, inadvertently overlooking other red flags that signaled a lack of attraction and common interests. While Texas brought the comfort of being not far from what I knew, I felt some of the same negative racial and misogynistic undertones professionally that I dealt with in Kansas. I needed more. I wanted more.

Then, in 2015, I was approached with an opportunity to join an amazing healthcare organization. It was terrifying because the career move would require me and my daughter to relocate to Northern California. There was a whirlwind of emotions as California was not the Midwest similarity during my first small move to Texas. However, I had enrolled in my second master's degree program and knew that this organization had all the characteristics I looked for as an individual and employee in both community and practice. It also helped that California seemed to match my free spirit more. I was ready for my ascent into the greatness I knew was in me. In April 2015 I accepted the job offer and set off to move halfway across the country to begin my new adventure. This is the same month my college love circled back and asked for a second chance.

Excitedly, I embraced this second chance at love and building a life with her, confident that she had grown during our time apart. The initial stages were promising, maintaining our compatibility, and enjoying the closeness with her amazing family. After a year of long-distance, she moved from Phoenix to Northern California to start our life. We enjoyed world traveling, basketball games, and a love for adventure. I had so much fun with the simple things we did together. We'd go to the farmer's market, the flea market, watch our weekly shows, and enjoy the fun of exploring California. Life was simple and satisfying. It felt good to speak to her mother every day and bond as her child. To have her dad be a support system. Life seemingly was heading in the right direction as I was accepted to the University of Southern California to study in a doctoral program and my career was satisfying. However, red flags soon emerged with my relationship, suggesting perhaps she hadn't grown as much as I had hoped. Recognizing that growth occurs at different rates, I learned the importance of patience in navigating her individual journey. I tried to give grace and allow her to grow own her own time. But at this point, I had learned the value of respect.

Challenges arose when I realized we weren't continuing to grow together, as I experienced the same situations as I did in college with her. By mid-2021, dealing with the frequent cheating constantly made me question my worth in the relationship. I couldn't fathom why she chose temporary attention over our shared foundation. None of the women offered anything of substance other than attention. I had to realize that it was her insecurities to deal with, not mine. Simultaneously, I realized the significance of protecting my peace and maintaining boundaries, especially in matters of respect.

Coping with the aftermath of frequent cheating involved me leaning on support from my best friends and even therapy. It is important for individuals to recognize their own worth and to understand that the actions of a partner do not define their value or potential for future happiness. After thoughtful consideration, I found her lack of growth consistently incompatible with mine, and my efforts to work through our differences were not met with equal energy. It was a difficult decision to walk away from a 15-year bond, but I knew prioritizing my own growth and well-being had to be more important. I knew I had so much in me to give. Ultimately, my decision to leave that relationship due to conflicting paths of personal growth was a deeply personal one.

THE THOUGHT OF DATING SOMEONE NEW AFTER ENDING A 15-YEAR BOND WAS OVERWHELMING

The thought of dating after that long commitment ended was overwhelming. But I had the support of my best friends who knew all the things I had gone through, that were both joyous and hurtful. They truly helped me navigate and understand that I was healed and able to give another person all of me genuinely. Since I am not exactly extroverted, I depended on one of my best friends a lot to encourage me to socialize. I ventured off into my newfound freedom, hopeful but not expecting anything. Also, I felt blessed in every other way. I was promoted at work. I was in my last year of my doctoral studies at the University of Southern California. Life was good!

Being in a good space in my life both mentally and emotionally truly allowed me to be open. I've always had a love-hate relationship with social media but that ultimately led me to my future wife. All it took was a simple *heart* from her on my profile to spark a mutual interest. I was nervous to say the least. I hadn't been on a first date with someone new in nearly a decade. Something about her made me feel so safe, respected, and protected from the very start. We had so much compatibility when it came to social interest, career, and life stories. Immediately I knew our connection was something special. I didn't have to fight for it and every feeling came naturally. We were in sync from the start. We loved and poured into one another equally. I also started to understand the importance of being equally yoked. She stayed true to her word. She was ready for all the things as I was. We were ready to see where life took us.

Life started to unfold in remarkable ways, and my heart burst with joy. I achieved another promotion at work, expanding my responsibilities, and found immense satisfaction in making significant professional contributions. Simultaneously, I graduated from the University of Southern California, and to my delight, my dissertation received a nomination for dissertation of the year. Adding to the whirlwind of happiness, she proposed to me right after graduation. Over the next year, we meticulously planned a dream wedding, surrounded by our dearest friends who stood by our side as we exchanged vows in June of 2023. The culmination of these achievements and personal milestones created a period of profound fulfillment in my life.

In her, I've found not just a confidante but a soulmate with whom I can share my entire life story, feeling a sense of safety and understanding. The appreciation she holds for me as a woman, mother, and wife is something I cherish deeply. Together, we have created a foundation of mutual respect and support.

It dawned on me that when you're building a life with the right person, there's an unstoppable synergy that propels you forward. I always say, I married the woman who loved me correctly the first time. Over the last three years of our journey together, my accomplishments have surpassed any other period in my life.

As I have so much to look forward to with my growing career, I am filled with gratitude. I have an incredible woman by my side, the warmth of family bonds, and the unwavering support of amazing friends.

If I were to give any advice it would be:

- Keep pushing.
- You will find your peace.
- Celebrate the small wins.
- Take hard times as lessons.
- Remember, it's just one chapter.

ABOUT DR. KACEE JONES

Dr. Kacee Jones is an established leader in the healthcare industry, with experience in multiple leadership positions. She completed her Doctoral of Education in Organizational Leadership at the University of Southern California with qualitative research on disparities in health access for marginalized individuals. Prior to that, she completed a Bachelor of Applied Sciences, Master of Management, and Master of Healthcare Innovation. Kacee shares a passion for dismantling systemic and systematic racism and protecting the freedoms of a woman's bodily autonomy. Through her life's journey, she has met some great friends and made unforgettable memories along the way. When she is not traveling the world or finding new doggies to pet, Kacee spends her time in California with her wife.

LinkedIn: *www.linkedin.com/in/dr-kacee-jones-172a07233*

17

KRISTINA CURTISS

FROM PEBBLES TO PROSPERITY: YOUR MINDSET SHIFT WILL CHANGE YOUR LIFE

AS A CHILD I WAS NEVER "GOOD ENOUGH"

*T*hrough all my brokenness, I learned to love all the pieces of me.

My childhood should have been idyllic: horseback riding on the beach every day after school on an island in the middle of the Atlantic Ocean.

The reality? I came from a broken, then blended family. I had limited time to spend with my father, stepmother, and siblings. What I missed the most was building a relationship with my father before he passed away.

I was a military dependent. This gave me the opportunity to experience diverse cultures, people, and traditions. Military families live on a modest income.

I was a "latchkey kid." At an early age, I learned responsibility and how to keep a strict schedule. My stepfather was controlling and abusive. He managed us. You said yes when he wanted to hear yes, no when he wanted to hear no, regardless of what the truth was, or you suffered severe punishment. My physical response when he raised his voice was to wet myself in fear of what was coming next. Nothing I did was ever good enough. I was seen as a burden and never celebrated. As a result, I fell in line.

Despite my upbringing, I had the drive to learn and experience new things. The abusive expectation of perfection caused panic attacks around something as simple as public speaking.

I was eight years old in a dress rehearsal for an Independence Day celebration. As others recited their lines and my turn got closer and closer, I felt it. The body's physical reactions do not align with logic. I became short of breath and almost fainted. My heart raced; I could not speak. This physical reaction continued to follow me through my life. It kept me from reaching my potential in public speaking, even simply reporting statistics in work meetings.

At the end of high school, my mom and stepfather again deployed overseas. I chose to stay behind this time so I would no longer be manipulated, controlled, or abused. My mom and stepfather gave me an offer to stay in the family home. But I would have to pay the house payment while going to college full-time. I did not care. I wanted to be independent. I worked two jobs and got roommates to pay their house payment. Eventually the stress became too much for me. I began to have symptoms of what many years later I found out was Crohn's Disease. I began to feel alone and on an island. This began to set the tone for my transition from my teenage years to my adult life.

MY RUSHED INDEPENDENCE SET THE STAGE FOR SERIAL POOR DECISION-MAKING

I met my first husband when I was in high school. I fell hard for a very charismatic young man who appeared to have it together. He moved into my house (one of my roommates). He was unfaithful when we dated, but I still agreed to marry him, after dating for seven years. In my mind, I had already made a commitment to be with him and that meant forever. He told his best friend at the time he was only marrying me because I was "manageable." The thing is, I was *manageable*. I bought a house. We started a family. After we had our first baby, he continued his unfaithful behavior.

I continued to work hard, and he continued to *manage* me. He did what he wanted, when he wanted, and with whom he wanted, with no respect for our family.

I remember one event that made me question what I had become and the path I had taken to get me to that place in life. I looked at the clock next to our bed, and he was still not at home. The clock read 2:00 a.m. Allegedly, he was still at work. I knew his work was closed many hours ago, so I started making calls. I thought maybe he was in a hospital or injured at the side of the road. Deep inside I knew he was not hurt; I knew he was with someone else.

I remember thinking to myself: *I do not want my children to allow themselves to be treated this way.* I knew at that moment I could not tolerate his behavior towards me, towards our family. That night I packed his suitcase, put it outside of our locked bedroom door and when he finally got home, I told him to leave. He tried everything to get me to allow him to stay in our home. He tried manipulating me, pleading with me, and begging me to take him back. He even said, "I don't want to live without you." Nothing moved me. I was resolved in that moment, as a mother to a young child now, to show her that we deserved respect. I knew no matter how difficult life would be without a partner, if I tolerated this behavior from him, my child could see it and feel it, and might somehow later tolerate it too. This was unacceptable to me.

THE START OF MY TRANSFORMATIONAL JOURNEY BEGAN IN CHURCH

As I looked to change my mindset, I knew I needed a new direction. I decided to join a church. At this church, I met a "Godly" man whose family was in the ministry. I thought to myself, *I am going to do this differently*. After about ten months, he asked me to marry him, and I accepted. He was great to my daughter and seemed to be very committed to us, our relationship, my newfound family, and the church community. In fact, I sold my house because we were going to build a house next to his parents.

However, while pregnant with my second daughter, he lost his job. I became the sole breadwinner again for my family. After having our baby, he only wanted to be with our daughter, and he did not try to get a job. I could sense his love for my first daughter dwindled and he acted as if she was a burden. He was very short tempered with her, and I often had to intervene. At that time, I was taking my newborn to work with me (I was still nursing) so his time with our daughter was quite limited. The money I got from the sale of my house became our replacement income and soon we were in debt. He was borrowing money from his parents and running up credit card debt. I became very sick working multiple jobs and trying to raise my kids with very little support from anyone. Reluctantly, he went back to work. At that time, our baby became very sick. She stopped breathing in the middle of the night and the doctors did not know what was ailing her. Shortly thereafter, I was diagnosed with Crohn's disease.

I remember the conversation I had with the doctor about my newly diagnosed condition. He told me it was the worst case he had seen in thirty years. Several rounds of medications and infusions failed, and they had to remove three feet of my intestines. On one of the days, post-surgery, I was lying in bed with thirteen staples in my stomach and sorting out my morning dose of the twenty pills prescribed by my physician. I decided at that moment I was not going to live this way any longer. I began to research my condition. I learned how to manage my condition through diet, stress reduction, and other means. I took matters into my own hands as I knew, again, for me and my kids, it was a matter of survival.

I KNEW I NEEDED TO CHANGE DIRECTION AGAIN SO I FURTHERED MY EDUCATION

I knew I needed another direction change. I was being dragged along by this thing called "life" and now I was receiving not only emotional and spiritual signs, but physical ones too. I decided to become my most successful self. I conducted research and decided to go back to school. I knew going back to school as the breadwinner, volunteering at church, taking care of myself and my chronically ill daughter, and fighting a custody and support battle would be difficult but I knew I had to take control.

Then things changed again.

One night around midnight my husband's phone chimed with a notification from an incoming text message. Groggily, he reached over and read the text. When I asked him who was texting him so late, he said it was his brother wishing him a happy birthday. I knew he was lying because his brother could not text due to a genetic condition. After he fell asleep, I forwarded the text to my phone. About a month later, we were out to celebrate a big accomplishment. Seven years of marriage. After an awkward dinner, we exchanged gifts. His gift to me was a necklace. My gift to him was a nude birthday picture from his lover. I told him don't bother denying it; the affair was confirmed by a private investigator. I told him that I would stay under a few conditions:

1. Stop cheating
2. Treat me and the kids with respect
3. Keep working (he had just started a job)
4. Get counseling

You are probably thinking, *why would you stay?* Partially the shame I was made to feel. This was the second man that had cheated, and my mom blames me for the first one cheating. She said if I had given him sex the way he wanted, he would not have cheated.

But the main reason I stayed is because our daughter nearly died under his parents' watch. Can you imagine coming home from a long day at work to your child gasping for air like a fish out of water? They neglected to administer her asthma medication. The one and only time this happened, I rushed her to the Urgent Care clinic. The nurses at the clinic insisted I take her to the emergency room because she was in respiratory distress. I had to stay with him until my daughter was old enough to self-administer her asthma medication. Her life depended on it.

Of the four conditions, he only managed to abide by two: keep a job and (technically) stop cheating. But he continued to treat my oldest daughter as if she were a burden and adopted additional bad behaviors. My youngest daughter was now old enough to self-administer. So, the kids and I moved to San Diego. The parting of ways was somewhat amicable, although devastating for our daughter. His version of our breakup was tearing her up inside. One night she screamed, "You did this, you made us move and made Daddy sad. He cries every time I see him, and it is your fault." She hated me. He controlled the narrative, and I would never say a bad word about him or his behaviors, at this point. I trusted that she would see it eventually.

When I arrived in San Diego, we moved into my mom's fifty-five plus, one-bedroom apartment. We were a family of four people, three dogs, and a bird. I was scared and did not know how I was going to make ends meet. My entire adult life I had supported myself and my family.

At that moment, I knew what I had to do and walked into the County Welfare office. I sat in the parking lot for at least an hour struggling to gain the courage to move my limbs to go in and admit that I needed help.

My mom was working in the healthcare industry and had been for years. She urged me to get a position in a small healthcare organization in San Diego. I knew nothing about the industry but decided I should try it. So, I did. I began by answering telephones and scheduling appointments for a cardiologist. I was constantly looking for my next opportunity.

Every time I hit any kind of a roadblock, I educated myself to be able to achieve the next position. Eventually, an opportunity was offered in the Information Technology (IT) project management that seemed exciting. I did research and decided to position myself for it. I applied and was accepted for the role.

I was fortunate to work for an organization that was rapidly growing and changing. There were many positions being offered and they were expanding. Soon, I changed roles again and I began working for the corporate IT Project Management Office. During this time, I was also fortunate to meet an unassuming mentor. My direct supervisor was a Project Management Professional (PMP), and he urged me to become PMP certified. He shared with me all the benefits of becoming certified and all the career opportunities that awaited me. I had already understood the value of furthering my education and how it had transformed my life.

For me, this was not enough. Not only did I get my PMP, I decided to also become certified in Microsoft Suite and other things along the way. My thirst for learning became unquenchable. I knew as a single mother I was setting myself up as a role model for my children. At the same time, my daughter's health was under control. My health was under control, and I was enrolling them in sports, acting, music, and whatever interests they expressed at the time. I was also able to manage the relationships with my ex-husbands. My mindset was positive, and my life trajectory was high.

DEATH REMINDED ME THAT LIFE IS PRECIOUS

I was very busy managing my life and started becoming comfortable feeling proud of myself and my accomplishments. I remember walking through the kitchen when the phone rang. It was my father and he rarely called. He informed me that he had stage 4 terminal cancer. I was speechless. He could sense my shock and, in my silence, he said, "Well, sis, we are not getting out of this life alive."

His end of life was full of ups and downs. The family rallied. We all worked to make his last days as meaningful for him as he had made our childhoods. After he passed, my niece summed my father up in a single sentence: "Bumpa was the man you ran from when you did something wrong and the man you ran to when you were afraid." She had great insight and perspective. Even though we sometimes disappoint him, he was there to protect you from the evils of this world. Over the next year as a family, we reflected on the death of my father and made attempts to stay connected over the distance that separated us. We met at our lake place yearly. When we were together it was like no time or distance ever separated us. We enjoyed fireside laughter, Nertz, and several harmless pranks that kept us close.

Then, my brother was diagnosed with melanoma that had returned with a vengeance and began to attack his lungs, heart, and brain. As brothers went, he was great. He was a wonderful man who put others above himself. He was the strong male figure to my kids. He picked them up from school, paid for summer camps, and gave art lessons to my youngest daughter. The cancer distorted his reality due to the twenty-plus tumors in his brain. This left us all heart broken. My kids were devastated, and their mental and physical health suffered. We all broke down.

OUR FAMILY CHALLENGES HAVE MADE US WHO WE ARE AND WE ARE STRONGER TOGETHER

My oldest daughter, who has given me permission to share this part of her story, was a healthy child in many ways, but in early adult-hood struggled with mental health challenges. She broke down after my brother passed away and after she experienced several other traumas in college. She escaped into her own reality. She thought she needed to stop the apocalypse. She left for Las Vegas, ran out of gas, and left her car and all other personal belongings in the middle of the freeway. Including her cell phone. She went missing. There is nothing like facing the idea that you may never see your child again. It was such a helpless feeling. After a day or so, she called me from a phone she borrowed from a restaurant. She hung up on me, so I called the restaurant back to get her location. I engaged all my resources and those of others close to me and began searching the streets. We finally tracked her down. I convinced her that we were going to the beach to rest a bit before she continued her journey. On the way to the beach, I pretended to have a Crohn's flare up so I could get her to the hospital. Once there, I was able to check her into the hospital. She was an adult at the time, and it was challenging to obtain information on how she was doing. The doctor and nurses could only talk to me if she said it was okay for them to do so. As you can imagine with an altered reality, she was not sure if I was a friend or foe. After about a week in a room in the Emergency Room, they finally got her to an in-patient facility where she was able to get the help and medication she needed. Today, she identifies with the pronouns they/them and is a healthy young person. They are looking for opportunities to advance in their career helping friends and family along the way.

My youngest has always faced health problems. Genetically, she was destined to struggle with simply breathing. We marshaled all the resources we could to help her throughout her life from when she was born through adulthood. We were finally able to determine she was born with a Cystic Fibrosis gene, which contributes to her symptoms. She struggled with depression, anxiety, and adjustment disorder. Watching my brother die only amplified these conditions. She struggled still to communicate with me and during a conversation she had with her father, the dots connected. She realized that it was not all my fault that our family was destroyed.

FROM VICTIM TO VICTOR: YOUR MINDSET SHIFT WILL CHANGE YOUR LIFE

As difficult as another loss was, we pulled together. I tried to be an example of being a victor and not a victim. It took years of my life to create a victor mentality and I still struggle sometimes. My kids often get frustrated at the lack of emotion I seemed to have towards, well, pretty much everything. Early on I implemented a rule of sorts. When we are sad or upset or devastated about something, we get a day. A day to be devastated, cry, vent, and dwell. Then, you need to shift your mindset. Of course, the thoughts and feelings do not just go away but we do not allow them to take over. Many people face challenges and devastation. It is what you do on the other end that will allow you to succeed.

I am immensely proud of my kids. I look to them for inspiration and new ways of thinking and doing things.

Who am I Now?

- **Victor** over being manageable and cheated on
- **Victor** over my mental and physical illness
- **Victor** over familial loss
- **Victor** over not being good enough

Action becomes reality. I take action to guide my life in directions that allow me to be victorious. Instead of dwelling in my circumstances, I research what opportunities are out there for me, for my kids, and for my career. I do uncomfortable things to push me to be a better me. I seek to understand others and build relationships where my life experiences can be leveraged to elevate others. I work every day to combat those things that hold me back. My passion today is to help others find their way through their challenges and guide others to be their most successful selves and to feed their own happiness.

I have grown, learned, and overcome.

I am a Project Management Professional at one of the nation's largest not-for-profit health plans. I serve as a champion for Equity, Diversity, and Inclusion (EID). I am the VP of Communications for the San Diego Chapter of the Project Management Institute. I speak at conferences guiding others to be good leaders, impart emotional intelligence, and move through organizational change. I encourage them to positively impact others around them and create successful business models.

I am a mother to two wonderful children and a daughter to an ailing mother. I am a sister that loves despite differences.

I am a victor because I have chosen to move from not feeling *good enough* to loving all of my brokenness despite whatever challenge I had to overcome.

I am a victor, and I am UNSTOPPABLE.

ABOUT KRISTINA CURTISS

As a child, Kristina traveled the world as a military dependent. She has two children whom she dedicated her life to supporting and inspiring. Kristina is a project management professional (PMP) in the healthcare industry. She works in the Strategic Consulting and Program Execution department at one of the largest healthcare organizations in the United States. In her current role she mentors employees and serves as the VP of Communications for the San Diego Chapter of the Project Management Institute (PMI). Her volunteer endeavors include coaching, Special Olympics, Equity, Inclusion, and Diversity, and Girl Scouts. Her passion is learning and sharing her knowledge and life experiences to guide others through challenging times. She lives by two fundamental philosophies. The first is "Being a victor is a choice" and "80/20 rule: 80% of Society Exist; 20 % Participate."

> **Email:** *krishappens@gmail.com*
> **Facebook:** *www.facebook.com/kristina.l.curtiss*
> **LinkedIn:** *www.linkedin.com/in/kristina-curtiss-*
> *90758764*

18

PHI TRAN

YOU HAVE WHAT IT TAKES

AT ELEVEN YEARS OLD, I CLUNG TO *HOPE* AS MY
STRATEGY FOR A BRIGHTER FUTURE.

*I*magine a confused eleven-year-old girl who follows
her parents, older sister, and younger brother onto an
airplane for the first time. She lands in a new country, at a busy
airport, Los Angeles, surrounded by new people, an incomprehensive
language, big, tall buildings, and a lot of fast vehicles.

That was me in 1993 when our family left Vietnam and the
communist government to immigrate to the United States in the
hope of a brighter future, pursuing the American dream. In my first
two years in America, there were a lot of challenges and unique experiences. We didn't have a lot of money, and we couldn't read, write,
speak, or understand English.

My mother had a cash-only job with the local clothing factory.
She would bring home clothes in a black bag for us to help her trim
strings from each piece of clothing and its buttons. I remember
helping her calculate how many buttons and pieces of clothes we

had completed, multiplied that by half a cent or a cent to total a small amount of money she made. She would give that paper to the owner of the shop. Sometimes they would pay her, and other times they would not. It was sad to see my mother struggling to find ways to help bring in extra money to help the family.

In 1996, my sister married and moved away to San Jose, California. My parents continued to struggle with English, and as we pressed on to navigate the new routine in America, I somehow became the default child and stepped into the adult role, assisting my family with everything. Throughout my teenage years, I learned to navigate this new world face on and pray for the best. I remember going with my father early in the morning every weekend to help him deliver the newspaper so it would be a little quicker for his day. My father was the only one to obtain a driver's license, so our family depended on him for transportation. As things came up, such as reviewing the mail, filling out various paperwork, and communicating with others on behalf of my parents, I did it. I would pretend to be my parents and answer questions. I stepped in and would be the voice on the phone when inquiring about the bank, the doctor's office, the social worker, or whoever we needed to talk to or answer. I accessed the ATM with my father's pin, paid with a card at the gas station, signed a check with his signature to pay bills, and applied for welfare, food stamps, and community resources. I grew up fast.

At school, I completed any paperwork needed and often wished to have the ability to be involved in extracurricular activities, if only they were free. Since we didn't have a lot of extra money, every night, we would walk around the neighborhood to exercise and collect cans and cardboard. My mother would have plastic bags, and we found cans from the trash and cardboard from the big trash can at Pizza Hut and Albertsons. Sometimes if we were lucky, the staff at Pizza Hut would give us the left-over pizza before they threw it in the trash, and that would be our treat.

My father had an old, mustard color van, and he would take out all the seats except the driver's seat so he could store as much cardboard and cans in the vehicle. Then he drove us to the recycling center, patiently got in line, waited at the weight area, and sold whatever was in the van. It was often not worth that much, and he used that as our treat. My father would take us to the Vietnamese sandwich shop, and we would get two *banh mi*, Vietnamese sandwiches, to share and celebrate.

My parents didn't have much money, so we never went to the malls, bought new clothes, traveled on vacation, and rarely ate out. However, we always had a roof over our heads, food on the table, clothes to wear, and parents present in our daily lives as we grew up. They were there reminding, supporting, pushing, and expecting us to excel in all we did. My parents had high expectations for all their children. They sacrificed a lot to restart their life in the United States and expected their children to keep the Vietnamese culture and tradition, and grow up well in appropriate role. I always knew the implied expectations my family had for me: pursuing higher education, having a professional career, staying close to family, and finding a respectful husband to build a family.

NAVIGATING ADULTHOOD

I am blessed with the love and support from my family and the opportunities America offers. I became the first person in my family to attend college and graduate with a bachelor's degree in nursing in the United States. In college, I had to overcome my fear of science and grammar so I could excel. I struggled with the perfection of the English language and often thought I was not as good as others. I realized English continued to be a challenge for me, but I needed to keep pushing forward and face it if I wanted to progress. I remember that I needed help multiple times regarding the difficult concepts in pathophysiology and pharmacology classes. I went to the tutoring center, sought help from friends, and tapped into various resources available to be successful in my courses.

I was thankful for the financial aid helping with tuition, but various other costs of being away from home presented themselves. I had two to three part-time jobs at one time to help pay for food, gas, parking, activities, and bills. Some of my jobs were as a cashier for concession stands, sales at Ann Taylor Loft, tutoring through the MESA program, and peer advisor for ASPIRE. These experiences allowed me to build my customer service skills and helped me realize areas I was good at or not. College gave me a lot more freedom away from my parents' expectations. I thrive on college but also made some poor decisions.

In 2005, I became the first female in the family to join the military and serve in the USAF. I had the opportunity to travel all over the world. I was stationed in California, England, Alaska, Florida, Alabama, Japan, and now in Virginia. I also surprised myself and overcame many military training events and exercises. I returned from deployment in Afghanistan with a better understanding of our military and international roles and another perspective of the female role in the Afghan community. The military continued to provide me the opportunity to serve patients and lead our airmen in various settings, at a hospital facility or in the back of an airplane. The opportunity to excel and the joy of leading our airmen to meet the mission has been abundant. In 2021, I was promoted to the rank of Lieutenant Colonel. I was now attending meetings where I might be the only Asian or female. I can now share my insights and advocate for others who may not have a voice at the table.

In 2016, one of my best friends passed away unexpectedly. We often talked about growing old together, and creating charity and opportunity that would serve the youth. When she passed away, I realized that there was no better time than now, and we might not know what would happen tomorrow. It ignited me to act and follow my passion for creating a charity serving youth in honor of Dorian. I created Fostering Our Youth Inc., a nonprofit organization serving youth with a group of amazing friends. We had similar beliefs about the importance of investing in our youth. In 2020, FOY officially launched and serves youth all over the nation with community outreach events, mentorship programs, and scholarship opportunities for high school seniors. We believe that our youth needs positive exposure and opportunities to find out what they want to pursue.

BREAKING POINTS AND REALIZATION

My life appeared like it was on the right track, professionally and personally. On April 12, 2021, I found out I was pregnant through a phone call from my provider, after a regular checkup appointment. At the time, I was stationed in Okinawa, Japan, served as a flight nurse, and was actively involved in my local community amid Coronavirus. The news of being pregnant, finding out the person I had been with was not who he appeared to be, and now having a child out of wedlock was terrifying. The thought of how to tell my parents and the disappointment from my family or the negative judgments from my culture was overwhelming. I was pregnant and would have to raise this child on my own, with a big fur baby, Chewie. Wow, I was not ready for all of this. I was scared like that eleven-year-old girl who arrived in the United States and felt alone, even knowing there were others around me.

For the first time, I thought about suicide, walking off into the ocean at the side of the lighthouse. No one would know, and everything would stop and be better. How could things change so drastically? The week before, I celebrated my 39th birthday with amazing friends, and all the excitement for the possibilities ahead. Now, my world flipped upside down. I would be on my own with this growing child in me, and the fear of facing my family and the many unknowns.

As I paused and prayed to God for help, I slowly acknowledged that it was scary to face this new event in my life, but I could do it. I needed to take it one day at a time. I called to follow up with the obstetrician provider and find out what additional steps and visits I needed to have. I had my community I could reach out to for help. I was at a stage in my life where I was financially stable to provide for this child, even if it was on my own. My career might take a detour, but the Air Force had programs that were set up to address their service members and pregnancy. I thought I could do this, and I had what it took within me to face this new challenge. I also had the strength within me to face my family and culture and press forward. I overcame many challenges in the past and come out on top and excelled. This would be another challenge.

It became a daily reminder to myself that I could face life as a single mom, raising this child, and create opportunities for this child to excel. I reminded myself I was enough, and a strong individual. I have the strength within me, the skill set and knowledge to access resources to better prepare for this baby's arrival. I had the community to support and pull me up whenever I needed it. I also realized that I could not live in the bubble of what my parents or family expected. Other people's perceptions or judgments of me are for them, and I could not live my life pleasing others. I would strive to live and serve others and be the best version of myself. Those who love me and accept me for who I am are those who I need or should keep in my corner. The rest are noises that will distract me if I allow them to.

I waited until the second trimester before I shared my pregnancy with my family. It was a new adventure, and I was trying hard to embrace this chapter of motherhood. As expected, my parents were very concerned and upset that I did not have a husband to help with raising a child. They also were concerned about how to share this news with the rest of the family. It took time but they finally came around to it. My parents wanted to make sure I took care of myself and the baby. They called me often to check up on the baby.

At this time, Japan had very strict rules about no travel due to COVID, and I didn't have family to come to help. However, I was blessed with some good friends who were local and able to assist me. I remember my mother sent me these ostrich eggs, as she believed I would need to eat them so my son would be smart and healthy. I ate three large ostrich eggs that my mom sent from California as a result. Maxx arrived in December 2021, and he was the perfect gift from God for me. Being a single mom and raising a young child on your own is no joke. I thought I was prepared, but oh no, I made mistakes, questioned my actions often, and prayed hard that I was doing the right thing for this baby. I was also so tired of busyness and lack of sleep. I heard often that motherhood is a privilege, but I sometimes wonder if I should have this privilege.

But wow, looking back now as Maxx is a two-year-old thriving in his wild toddler stage, I am amazed at myself.

I'm so glad I did not act on my suicidal thoughts and I'm here to witness my blessings. I realize that we, as women, have so much strength, heart, and resilience within us. We were built to adapt to all the challenges life hands to us. We need to be strong, smart, kind, loving, fearless, and resilient while facing struggles and come out better on the other side. We have it within us all of these times.

For me, all the hardships and challenging experiences from childhood prepared me for who I am today. My various accomplishments are reminders for me of the result of hard work and dedication. All the good and bad from the past are part of who I am today. I have what is needed to face life head-on, coming out on top. If I'm not winning it, I will learn and grow from the experience. I also learned that I do not need the approval of my family for everything. My family still loves me and wants the best for me. I now try to live my authentic best version of myself daily. I work hard to build a world where Maxx can flourish and grow into who he is meant to be. I learned that many others may struggle or face the same challenges as my past experiences.

I want to shed a small glimpse of my life, and let you know that I overcame adversity with the grace of God and my community.

You, wherever you are, could too if only you trust yourself and know you have what it takes.

You are enough and favored.

You deserve love and respect.

When challenges come your way—and they will—pause, take deep breaths, move one step at a time, and believe in yourself.

Don't be discouraged but know that you have been prepared for this day.

You will figure it out and you will handle it better than the last time.

Seek out support from your community for help.

You can be successful, powerful, and unstoppable in your own space.

I hope my story inspires you and gives you a boost to your self-esteem.

I hope it reminds you that you are worth way more than you know.

ABOUT PHI TRAN

Born in Vietnam and raised in California, Phi is a trailblazing single mother and dedicated Air Force nurse officer. She balances her career with nurturing her young son, Maxx, and her dog, Chewie. Phi's commitment to service extends to her community through initiatives like Fostering Our Youth Inc. (FOY), where she engages in community outreach, mentors and supports young children. She also volunteers with Legacy Flight Academy, introducing youth to aviation. Recognized for her professional achievements, Phi received the President's Lifetime Achievement Award and the 2021 Agent of Change Award. Phi's experiences professionally and personally encapsulate the spirit of service, empowerment, uplifting others and paying it forward. She also believes representation matters and the power of stories sharing and its impact to others. This was shared through her collaboration with Chief Vasquez (retired) to publish *A Different Shade of Blue: Stories by Asian American and Pacific Islander United States Air Force Airmen*, highlighted 48 military individuals and their experiences. Phi's tireless efforts to uplift others and create positive change serve as a testament to her character and commitment to making the world a better place for all.

Websites: www.fosteringouryouth.org
www.legacyflightacademy.org
Facebook: www.facebook.com/fosteringouryouth

SANET VAN BREDA

DREAM CATCHER

"If your WHY is big enough, you could do anything, you can do everything!"

— MY GOLDEN NUGGET

Unbreakable, Unbelievable, Unstoppable... wow, what do these words have in common? Me!

At the end of each day, I ask myself, "Sanet, did you leave your sparkle in someone's heart and memory today?" And with my whole heart, I believe that I do. I really do. It's funny, I feel a surge of love every time I repeat those words, reminiscent of the two "I dos" I uttered—once when I got married thirty-four years ago, and again atop the Empire State Building when I received a call to action from God. I had fervently prayed for the opportunity to pick up my grandsons from school every day, to be the kind of grandmother who dances, plays, and nurtures their imagination for as long as possible. This desire, deeply rooted in my heart, was now being answered by a journey I had been on with God for the past few years. I was ready and open to whatever He had in store for me.

Standing in line to enter the Empire State Building, the atmosphere was filled with cheerfulness and happiness. Despite it being six days into 2022, people were still wearing their masks with a sense of joy. I eagerly awaited our turn to go inside; it had been a lifelong dream of mine ever since I watched "An Affair to Remember" with Cary Grant and Deborah Kerr. Back in 1976, South Africa had just begun its television journey, and I can still remember our first set —a simple black-and-white model. In the early '90s, one of my favourite movies, "Sleepless in Seattle," featured an unforgettable romantic scene atop the Empire State Building. As I stood in line, I couldn't help but wonder: would the view be as breathtaking as it was in the movies? And perhaps, just maybe, would I encounter my favourite movie moment come to life?

The history and interconnectedness of the Empire State Building's journey to the top was truly amazing. Even the elevator operator wished me a wonderful experience as we ascended. As I reached the summit, the scene before me took my breath away, and I could feel my core temperature drop by ten degrees. Feeling frozen, I leaned against the wall and looked upward, wondering where the warmth emanated from. Suddenly, beams of redness enveloped me, as if they were saying, "Lady from South Africa, you are really not dressed for New York's January weather. Let us warm you a bit." Grateful for the unexpected warmth, I hesitated to wear my husband's thick archery jacket, which proudly displayed "South Africa Archery" on the back. After all, South Africa had recently been removed from the red list, having been labelled as the originating country for the Omicron virus back in November 2021.

Standing underneath the beaming sunlight, I offered gratitude to my beautiful God for the love and grace He bestowed upon me on the 6th of April 2019. That day marked a pivotal moment—a point of no return—when I made the decision to embrace life rather than succumb to its weight. It was a profound shift, igniting a commitment to move more than I consumed. Dancing my Forever Song, "Walking on Sunshine," every day and some days five to eight times. What followed were months and years of the most tumultuous roller coaster ride of my life. I clung to God's promise that He would support me, while I, in turn, vowed to do whatever it took to shed the weight of an entire person. Some days were easier than others; some were impossibly heavy, requiring me to navigate through each minute, each moment, with relentless determination.

The battles waged within my mind seemed endless, echoing doubts of whether this struggle would ever cease. Yet, despite the relentless onslaught of doubt and the mind games I endured, I pressed on. I persevered, steadfastly following my Oumie and Zander Plan (Oumie being "granny" in my home language Afrikaans, and Zander being my grandson). Two and a half years later, I emerged victorious—I had shed the weight of an entire person. But it wasn't just pounds I lost; I gained so much more: strength, resilience, and a profound sense of pride in myself and my ability to take action, speak out, and bravely face challenges. Self-respect, self-love, self-discipline, and self-belief—all the "self" elements—became integral parts of my life story and my mission to share with the world. I learned that by infusing every day with self-love and mindfulness, you can accomplish anything, you can conquer everything. My incredible journey and transformation are detailed in my book *Flight of the Monarch: The Hero Inside Me.*

Standing in the warmth of the beaming heaters, I gazed down at the buildings and the tranquil Hudson River, enveloped in the symphony of laughter echoing from those who were also experiencing this breathtaking panorama. With my heart overflowing with longing, I closed my eyes and offered a prayer to God, beseeching Him for a miracle to fulfil my deepest wish: to be reunited with my beloved grandsons. My soul yearned to live each day with purpose, to serve others in every way possible. Over the past five years, I have found my voice and embraced my worth, experiencing a profound transformation that has altered the course of my life forever. My greatest desire is for others to encounter this miraculous journey of self-discovery and empowerment that I have been blessed with. I am driven by a passion to showcase the inherent value of every individual, to assure them that their stories are significant and worthy of celebration.

God answered, "Open your eyes; you will inspire so many people around the world." As I opened my eyes, my heart nearly stopped at the sight before me. It wasn't the buildings or the Hudson River; it was millions of people looking at me. Overwhelmed, I forgot to breathe, tears streaming down my face. "Yes, my beautiful Lord, I am ready to fulfil Your God-given plan," I whispered. "Thank you for trusting me. I do... I will take action every day." With blurry focus, a gentleman approached, asking if I was okay. Nodding, I wiped my tears and snot with the underside of my blouse. As I looked into his eyes, he reassured me, "Everything is going to be okay." In Afrikaans, he added, "Alles wat jy daar sien gaan waar word!" Shocked, I realized his words affirmed my vision. Tears flowed again, for the second time in three years, as God silently promised my dreams of becoming a hands-on granny and living in my purpose, Serving with Love, would come true. With this incredible miracle unfolding before me, I am compelled to step up and transform my vision into reality, making my dream of creating my vision "To be earth's most heart-centred brand to provide experience to fill the world with love, joy and happiness!"

In the first sentences, I have used three words, and the first two words show you what happened and why I wanted to become UNSTOPPABLE.

With my newfound truth and understanding, I've come to realize that every encounter with another person holds profound meaning. It's an opportunity for me to leave a glimmer of my own sparkle and to experience the unique brilliance of others—their wisdom, dreams, and individuality—each and every day. Embracing authenticity and staying true to myself, I continue on my God's Quest, on a journey filled with gratitude during my six-month stay in America. I'm deeply grateful to my sister and brother-in-law for graciously hosting me during my travels, allowing me the space to connect with others and explore new horizons.

In this spirit of connection and empowerment, I took the first step towards manifesting my vision by transforming my beloved Diamond Beauties Forever ladies' group. What began as a WhatsApp group of seventy-nine women evolved into a private Facebook community—a sacred space where ladies come together to inspire and uplift one another through life's highs and lows. It's a testament to the power of sisterhood and the resilience of the human spirit, where women from all walks of life can find solace, support, and strength in each other's presence. As I witness the bonds of sisterhood deepen and the flames of inspiration ignite within our group, I am reminded of the profound impact that one small step can have. By listening to the whispers of my heart and taking action, I've created a ripple effect of love and empowerment that extends far beyond my wildest dreams. It's a beautiful reminder that when we align with our true selves and trust in the guidance of a higher power, miracles unfold, and our vision becomes reality.

What steps could you take when you want to become Unstoppable? I have a Miracle five-step plan that I would love to share.

5STEPS2BEUNSTOPPABLE

Step 1 - Clarify Your Why

Your why is the driving force behind your actions, the fuel that propels you forward even when faced with challenges. Take a moment to deeply reflect on what truly motivates you, what ignites your passion, and what you're willing to do anything and everything for. In both of my transformative plans—Oumie and Zander Plan (Lifestyle Change) and now in my SLIM Plan—I have anchored myself in my why. I've defined my goals and aspirations, painting a vivid picture of the end result I strive to achieve.

As you set your sights on your own journey, consider your principles and values. They serve as your guiding compass, keeping you aligned with your true path. Imagine your journey as a bridge spanning from where you currently stand to where you aspire to be. Envision the Golden Gate Bridge in San Francisco stretching out before you—a magnificent testament to possibility and adventure. Though the path ahead may seem daunting from your vantage point, trust that once you cross the bridge, you'll behold a breathtaking vista that awaits you on the other side.

Step 2 - Dream in 3D

One of my favourite steps on the journey to becoming unstoppable is to dream in 3D. This transformative practice costs nothing and yet yields priceless rewards. Over the past three years, I've discovered the power of dreaming with all my senses, bringing my visions to life in vivid detail. Picture yourself in a grand movie theatre, the screen illuminated before you. You're not just a passive observer; you're the leading actress, experiencing every emotion, sensation, and moment within the film.

As the story unfolds,you feel the rush of excitement, the warmth of love, and the thrill of adventure coursing through your veins. Then, with a shift in perspective, you step outside the confines of the screen, immersing yourself in the world you've created. It's akin to stepping into a painting and exploring its depths from every angle. (One movie that depicted this immersive experience was "Inception," where characters entered dream worlds within dream worlds, blurring the lines between reality and imagination.)

Step 3 - Designing your Blueprint

To design your blueprint for success, it's essential to set SMART goals. Break down your vision into specific, measurable, achievable, relevant, and time-bound objectives. By doing so, you provide clarity and direction to your journey, enabling you to focus your efforts and track your progress effectively. For example, if your ultimate goal is to start your own business, your SMART goals might include tasks such as completing a business plan within three months, securing funding within six months, and launching your product or service within a year. Each goal is clearly defined, with measurable milestones that guide you towards your overarching vision.

Another crucial element of designing your blueprint is cultivating a growth mindset. Embrace challenges as opportunities for growth rather than setbacks. Adopt a mindset that views failure as a steppingstone to success and believes in your ability to learn and improve. This shift in perspective empowers you to overcome obstacles with resilience and perseverance. Instead of being discouraged by setbacks, you see them as valuable learning experiences that propel you forward. With a growth mindset, you approach each challenge with optimism and determination, confident in your ability to adapt and thrive in any situation.

Continuously seeking knowledge and developing new skills is a cornerstone of designing your blueprint for success. Invest in personal and professional development opportunities that are relevant to your goals. Whether it's taking courses, attending workshops, or seeking mentorship, prioritize learning and growth as integral components of your journey. For instance, if your goal is to advance in your career, you might pursue certifications or training programs that enhance your skills and expertise in your field. By expanding your knowledge base and honing your abilities, you position yourself for success and open doors to new opportunities.

Step 4 - It's All in the Action

In the pursuit of your goals, taking consistent action is paramount. Break your goals down into smaller, manageable tasks and commit to taking action towards them every day. While progress may seem slow at times, each step forward brings you closer to your vision. By consistently showing up and putting in the work, you build momentum and make steady progress towards your desired outcome. Whether it's dedicating a set amount of time each day to work on your goals or completing specific tasks, consistency is key to achieving success.

As you navigate across your Golden Gate Bridge towards becoming unstoppable, it's essential to embrace resilience. Setbacks and obstacles are inevitable along the way, but it's how you respond to them that matters most. Cultivate resilience by bouncing back from setbacks, learning from failures, and adapting to change. Instead of allowing challenges to derail you, view them as opportunities for growth and learning. Embracing resilience enables you to persevere in the face of adversity, ultimately strengthening your resolve and fortifying your commitment to your goals.

Surrounding yourself with positive, supportive individuals is essential for staying motivated and inspired on your journey. Seek out mentors, coaches, and peers who believe in your potential and encourage your growth. Surrounding yourself with a supportive network provides you with valuable guidance, encouragement, and accountability. Whether it's seeking advice, sharing successes and challenges, or simply receiving words of encouragement, having a supportive community by your side can make all the difference in staying focused and motivated towards achieving your goals.

Step 5 - Celebrate Small and Big Achievements

Celebrating both the small and big achievements along the way is a crucial step in the journey towards becoming unstoppable. With each milestone reached, I weave celebrations into my goal-planning process. Whether it's something as simple as treating myself to an ice cream cone or as grand as splurging on a new dress, I ensure that I acknowledge and honor my progress and accomplishments. It's not just about celebrating the end goal but also embracing the journey itself—the trials, triumphs, and everything in between.

As I pursue my goals with unwavering determination, I recognize the importance of prioritizing self-care. Taking care of my physical, mental, and emotional well-being is essential for sustaining momentum and resilience on my journey. I make it a priority to engage in self-care activities that recharge and rejuvenate me, enabling me to show up as my best self each day. Whether it's spending time in my hydroponics garden, or simply taking a few moments to meditate, practicing self-care allows me to nurture myself and maintain balance amidst life's demands.

In the ever-changing landscape of life, remaining flexible and adaptive is key to navigating challenges and seizing new opportunities. I embrace an open-minded approach, willing to adjust my plans and strategies as needed to overcome obstacles and pursue my goals. By staying flexible and adaptive, I empower myself to respond effectively to change and uncertainty, ensuring that I can adapt to whatever comes my way with resilience and grace.

Finally, it's important to acknowledge and celebrate your wins, no matter how small. Each achievement, no matter how seemingly insignificant, is a testament to your progress and dedication. By recognizing and celebrating your successes, you reinforce positive habits and bolster your confidence, fueling your momentum on the unstoppable journey ahead. Whether it's sharing your achievements with loved ones, treating yourself to a special reward, or simply taking a moment to reflect and express gratitude, celebrating your wins is a powerful way to honor your journey and inspire continued growth and success.

The greatest lesson I've learned on my journey to becoming unstoppable is this: when I wholeheartedly commit myself to a cause, fueled by unwavering determination rooted in my why, I am unstoppable. Through consistency, perseverance, and an unshakeable belief in myself, I've come to realize that the realm of possibilities knows no bounds. As I continue to embrace each challenge as an opportunity for growth, celebrate both small victories and significant milestones, and nurture my mind, body, and spirit with self-care, I stand emboldened by the profound truth that anything I set my mind to is within my reach.

Your power and wisdom are always within you; you simply need to delve into the depths of your heart and soul. Begin with your purpose, your why, and dare to dream big, bold dreams. Then, take decisive action to become the person you aspire to be. For me, this journey of becoming means embodying the voice of millions, creating space and platforms for extraordinary souls to illuminate our world with their brilliance, wisdom, and transformative stories. Through my Your Voice TV Network, Diamond Moments Magazine, and summits, I strive to empower individuals to share their voices and shine brightly, making a meaningful impact on the lives of others.

As we stand united in our pursuit of greatness, let us remember to dream BIG, dream BOLD, and keep our own DREAM Catcher in sight at all times. What may once have seemed impossible now stands within our grasp, waiting to be realized. Let us embrace the power of possibility, the magic of hope, and the beauty of resilience. With every step we take, let us illuminate the path for others, igniting a ripple effect of transformation and joy. So, dear friend, go forth with courage, with passion, and with love. Believe in the extraordinary potential that resides within you, and know that together, we can turn dreams into reality. Mwah!

ABOUT SANET VAN BREDA

Sanet Van Breda is the voice of millions, offering platforms for extraordinary souls to shine their brilliance and share transformative stories across various mediums, including Your Voice TV Network, Diamond Moments Magazine, Soul Diamond Publishers, and MWAH Production. Her mission is dedicated to empowering communities, particularly Diamond Beauties Forever and Tanzanite Heroes.

Website: *www.selflove4me.com*
Email: *slim@selflove4me.com*

ABOUT FOSTERING OUR YOUTH INC.

Fostering Our Youth Inc. (FOY) is a 501(c)(3) non-profit organization that was forged out of a deep calling to inspire and mentor upcoming generations. We are a group of volunteers who are dedicated to helping and supporting youth around the world. We have overcome demanding obstacles, and we want to pass on our experiences and lessons learned.

In 2016, our founders' dear friend, Ms. Dorian Gregory, passed away unexpectedly. Ms. Phi Tran and Mr. Eric Johnson shared Dorian's love for helping others, especially children. Dorian was an amazing individual, an operational room nurse, and a veteran who was full of life, kindness, love for her family and the will to serve others. In her honor and the realization of the benefits of positive role models because of their struggles navigating adolescence, teenage, and young adult years, Phi and Eric created FOY. After three years of molding and collaborating with those who shared their stories of personal challenges, experiences, and achievements, FOY became a family and a reality. Together we spark young kinds to strive for excellence in all they do. Making live changes in local and global communities is the way forward for FOY.

Our Mission: Mentor, Inspire, Connect, and Outreach (MICO)

Our Vision: With the Outreach Tiers focus, we want to build a better future and inspire all youth regardless of their background and circumstances by exposing them to positive influences, opportunities, and mentorship.

FOY focuses on three areas: Community Outreach, Mentorship, and Scholarship.

Community Outreach Tier:

A unique aspect of FOY's outreach is that it can happen at any time or anywhere due to its inspirational intent and common-ground approach. FOY collaborates with local businesses to provide free events for youth, focusing on exposing them to positive interactions and opportunities. We emphasize that through hard work, dedication, and resilience, all things are possible.

Mentorship Tier:

The FOY mentorship program's vision is to expose underrepresented youth to positive influences and opportunities to empower them to have a bright future. It is a six-month effort that connects a youth (mentee) with a FOY mentor to provide support and guidance. We tailor mentorship to include virtual/distance mentoring rather than in-person mentoring. The mentorship program focuses on financial literacy, communication/public speaking skills, resilience skills, and education/career goals.

Scholarship Tier:

FOY offers scholarships of $1000 each to high school graduates excelling in academic, community development, and volunteerism. We also partner with donors to create additional scholarships to serve our youth. Our first partnership scholarship is Dorian Gregory Memorial, focusing on a nursing major. Our second partnership scholarship is Joel Van Fears, focusing on a degree in STEM and attending a historically black college or university.

We want to especially thank our current staff, business partnerships, and donors for their dedication to building a brighter future for the youth worldwide through time and monetary investing in Fostering Our Youth.

Board of Directors:

President: Phi Tran
Vice President: Eric Johnson Jr.
Community Outreach Director: Vielkis McLeod
Mentorship Director: Paul Wilson
Scholarship Director: Nicholas Williford
Treasurer: Kristine Pulido
Secretary: Debra Lighten

Committee Members: Elizabeth Povroznik, Keith Kitagawa, Lloyd Houk, Angele Devezin, Daniel Vo, Arturo Tovar, Kenneth Thomas, Amanda Turcotte, Yvette Bivins, Megan Nguyen, Tomeka Jones, Shannon Early-Rice, Russell Lewis, Stefanie Diedrich

We would love more engagement and advocacy of our efforts. You can stay engaged with us via the following links.

Website: *www.fosteringouryouth.org*
Facebook Page: *www.facebook.com/fosteringouryouth*
Instagram: *@fosteringouryouth*

ABOUT AMA PUBLISHING

AMA Publishing is an international, award winning publishing company that champions the stories of entrepreneurs who are trailblazers, innovators, and instigators.

Forbes has said that, *"AMA Publishing is helping women reshape the future of publishing."*

We would love to help you tell your story. We have helped thousands of people become international, bestselling authors through our courses, multi-author books, and as solo authors.

Your story, it's ready to be told.

Website: *www.amapublishing.co*